# daditude

# ADVANCE PRAISE

"Chris Erskine hits nothing but home runs. His work is replete with wit, context, perception, and almost always a healthy dose of compassion. I've loved his columns for years. You will, too."

— Al Michaels, legendary sportscaster

"No one writes columns like these. They have the warmth of family life columns from the sixties, but they are fully modern and encompass so much of life as we live it right now. . . There is a haunting doubleness to these essays—always there is something elegiac. They are about the passing of time in your own family, but they stand also for a passing kind of American life."

— Caitlin Flanagan, contributing editor of *The Atlantic* and former staff writer at *The New Yorker*

# daditude

## *the* JOYS *&* ABSURDITIES
## *of* MODERN FATHERHOOD

——

### CHRIS ERSKINE

COLUMNIST FOR THE *Los Angeles Times & Chicago Tribune*

PROSPECT PARK BOOKS

PROSPECT
· PARK ·
BOOKS

Published by Prospect Park Books
www.prospectparkbooks.com

Distributed by Consortium Books Sales & Distribution
www.cbsd.com

Library of Congress Cataloging in Publication Data is on file with the Library of Congress
Erskine, Chris | Daditude
   Humor; parenthood/fatherhood; essays; family life
ISBN: 9781945551307
Ebook ISBN: 9781945551314

Design & layout by David Ter-Avanesyan
Printed in Canada

*To dads everywhere*

# CONTENTS

# LET ME EXPLAIN . . .

There are certain things you can count on. Everything is better with bacon on it. Whipped cream is best right out of the can. Yogurt is a lousy substitute for sour cream.

And laughter is life's secret sauce.

Of course, I'm indebted to my family—the coal that stokes my furnace, privately and professionally. I'm also fortunate for the encouragement of readers, friends, and colleagues.

"No one writes columns like these," wrote Caitlin Flanagan, a contributor to *The Atlantic* and former staff writer at *The New Yorker.* "They have the warmth of family life columns from the sixties, but they are fully modern and encompass so much of life as we live it right now . . . There is a haunting doubleness to these essays—always there is something elegiac. They are about the passing of time in your own family, but they stand also for a passing kind of American life."

Obviously, she has me confused with someone else.

Who will like this book? Quiet souls like me who follow jazz or linger too long over lighthouses.

But also wise guys who enjoy belly laughs and Chevy Chase pratfalls. Those who appreciate oversized cheeseburgers, tight spirals, and the majesty of a cocktail-party quip.

Who else will like this collection on fatherhood, culled from my weekly newspaper columns? Dads and moms. Sons and daughters. Dogs and cats.

Pretty much everybody will like this book is really what I'm hoping. As a bonus, family members, friends and I have added footnoted commentary to many of the columns. These "tailpieces" give a little insight into what went on.

The collection of fifty columns begins with us bringing our youngest home from the hospital fifteen years ago and ends with more hospital scenes, dramatically different and our biggest challenge ever.

My own father used to say: "If you have kids, you have everything." To that, I would add health. If you have health, you have everything as well.

I hope you devour this book shamelessly, as if no one's watching, like a big gooey pizza at midnight.

Or, as with a favorite photo you tuck away in a drawer, you look at it when you need a lift and a shot of life's special sauce.

Enjoy.

# MILESTONES

# BRINGING THE BABY HOME

*December 18, 2002*

The first mistake most new parents make is to take the baby home, leaving behind a hospital full of professionals.

"What's the rush?" I ask.

"I want to go home," my wife says.

"But you've been home before," I say. "You know what that's like."

"Let's go," she says.

So I pull away from the curb the way fathers of newborns always pull away from hospitals, as if driving a load of champagne across rail tracks.*

"Watch that bump," my wife says.

"Got it," I say.

They are in the back seat, mother and son, wrapped in blankets against the December chill. More blanket than baby, there's almost nothing to this infant boy. At three days old, he's as light as a passing thought.

"You sure this car seat's tight?" my wife asks.

"I double-checked," I tell her.

She double-checks my double-checking. Moments like that make a long marriage worthwhile.

"Told you," I say.

"Just checking," she explains.

And off for the rest of his life we go, onto the freeway, where I drive the speed limit. Ever driven the speed limit in LA? Of course not. It's unsafe.

Little old ladies in Buicks pass us as if we're standing still. Trucks pass us. Electric cars. Seagulls. Women pushing strollers. Squirrels. Virtually everything in LA is whooshing past us.

"Not too fast," my wife says.

"See that, a Vega," I tell her. "A Vega just passed us."

"Look, he's blowing bubbles," she says, admiring her second son.

The birth was easy. There were painkillers then. Morphine. Demerol. And that was just for the fathers. The mothers got a little help, too.

"The doctor said that during the circumcision, his heartbeat didn't change at all," my wife says proudly.

"The doctor's?"

"No, the baby's," she says.

In a hospital, even a baby senses that things will turn out well. The people are prepared there. A calm efficiency pervades the place.

Now we're headed home, where calm efficiency disappeared in 1983, replaced by a sort of martial law intended to keep things orderly. There are curfews. Chains of command. Constant surveillance. Into this tender truce, we bring the baby.**

"They're home!" the little girl screams.

"Someone get the camera," says the older daughter.

"Cheese!" says the boy.

I bring in the flowers. I stow away the baby gear. I stay clear of the baby until there's some sort of septic issue that threatens the public health.

"Can you change him?" my wife asks.

"Into what?"

"His diaper," she says. "Can you change his diaper?"

It's been a good ten years since I've changed a baby, and when I say "good" I mean in the sense that I didn't have to change a diaper. For even back then, I was never very good at it.

So I set this new baby on the changing table, where he looks at me skeptically. You can almost read his thought balloons.

"Who are you again?" the baby wonders. "Where's the person with the functioning bosom?" That sort of thing.

"Hold still," I tell him.

He wiggles like a trout.

"You'll fit in fine here," I say.

The baby soon finds that being dressed by his father is akin to the birth experience, only worse.

For example, I can't seem to thread this kid's tiny hand through a shirt hole the size of a nostril. I grab and try to guide his hand through. He pulls away.

I try bringing the hole to the arm instead of the arm to the hole. No luck. I'd have better luck building a microcircuit with my lips.

"Where's his other sock?" asks the little girl.

"What other sock?"

"He's missing a sock," she says.

The world has plenty of socks—more socks than people, probably. More socks than attorneys.

But the loss of this one particular sock concerns us all. It's a symbol of frustrations to come.

Finally, we find the sock. Tiny as a thimble, it had slipped off the changing table, where the dog sniffed it out of sight. When I place a fresh one on his foot, it fits him loose. Lord, he's tiny.

"I've had cheeseburgers bigger than you," I tell him softly.

"Do you always think of food?" he wonders.

"Pretty much all the time," I say.

It's three in the afternoon. Darkness nears. Long nights. And there are many hours to go before we sleep.

\* **The little guy responds:**
*Please drive like that again. You drive too fast!*

\*\* **Posh adds:**
*The baby arrived a week before my birthday. Best holiday gift ever.*

# HOMEMADE SOUP, THE FIRST FIRE . . .

*November 3, 2005*

It's a fall day. A perfect day. Some complain that the afternoon air is too cool, but we've been sun-blasted hot here in the foothills for five long months. The cool feels good. Like brushing your teeth. Like a snowy kiss.

We need this hint of winter. It herds us toward each other in substantial ways. Toward a kitchen, where soup is simmering.

Yes, I'm making soup. I would make soup even if I didn't like soup. I turn on a football game, I chop some garlic, I boil some water and add a ham bone and some beans. Soup. It's that easy.

The people I live with, the ones I care about most, are not around. It is pleasantly quiet in ways it seldom ever is. You can hear the floorboards creak. The snap of a brass lockset in a good heavy door. House sounds. In the corner, a dog snores softly.

I pour a soft drink over shaved ice. I turn down the sound on the game and put on a Todd Rundgren album. It reminds me of college and the papers I didn't finish. Turns out that finishing stuff is overrated.

"I'll come around to see you once in a while,

Or if I ever need a reason to smile . . ."

On TV, the Giants and Cowboys are going into overtime. Somebody loses a helmet. A place kicker practices into a net. I have seen this a thousand times, the closing seconds of a tight ballgame. In heaven, all games go to overtime.

During a Dallas drive, I sample the soup. Needs salt. I add salt. Needs oregano. I add oregano. I had a bad experience with oregano once. It was worse than being mugged. I sprinkle it carefully. Cooking with oregano is like cooking with gunpowder.

In the bedroom, a teenager stirs. He hasn't been sleeping; he's been hibernating. He is a Zits cartoon. He is a James Dean movie. I offer him soup. He scratches his head and mumbles, "I-dunno-I-think-I'd rather-have-cereal." Kids.

I make a fire. It is the first fire of fall, the best fire of fall. I throw in a couple of pinecones to juice the air, and an issue of *The New Yorker* that I didn't much care for. Overrated, *The New Yorker.* Too long. Too repetitive. Like a friend of a friend who won't leave.

The people I live with return. They have been out buying a homecoming dress for the little girl. It's a mystery why a little girl needs a homecoming dress since she's still a little girl and will always be my little girl. I refuse to let her grow up. Kids are the opposite of wine. They don't always improve with age.

In the meantime, the toddler sits in the living room, content to play with the dust particles floating in a shard of November sunlight.

"You should see my dress, Daddy," the little girl says.

It's a green dress, the color of martini olives. Macy's, probably. Or maybe the National Guard.

"I don't know if I like this dress," she says, trying it on again.

In my experience, there are two times a woman tries on a dress, in the store and again at home. One has nothing to do with the other. The fact that she liked it in the store will have absolutely no bearing on whether she likes it in her bedroom.

"That dress looks adorable," her mother insists.

"I hate my hair," the little girl says, though it is the color of chestnuts and hangs like expensive linen.

There is the threat of tears. The little girl hates her hair so much, they go out looking for another dress.*

"I love her hair," I tell the soup.

"We can't play this game anymore . . ." says Todd Rundgren.

There'll be soup here when they get home. And a fire. And a football game. Bread, warm from the oven, sprinkled with Parmesan cheese.

The kids will come into the house, since it's too cool and drizzly to stay outside, or to go to the beach, or to hang at some friend's Jacuzzi—all the usual activities that lure children away from the house in warmer months, which are glorious but disruptive. Fun but fractured.

Today, instead, they'll come inside because the house smells of pumpkins and soup, like a country diner on a frosty day. Like a family cabin in the woods.**

That's why we like fall.

**The columnist adds:**
*\* My favorite line.*
*\*\* In case you had any doubts, I'm a dork.*

# YEAH! A BEAGLE PUPPY

*March 25, 2004*

Best moment with the new puppy? When the baby pulled his pacifier out, put it in the dog's mouth, then put it back in his own mouth. That sort of thing can't be good for a little dog.

"Isn't this puppy cute?" my wife says.

"Just keep him off the carpets," I say.

The lovely and patient older daughter is back for spring break, with bags of dirty laundry, a new puppy, and that crème brûlée torch she uses to weld rich, eggy desserts. God bless these college kids for their resourcefulness and lack of forethought.

"She's a puppy raising a puppy," I tell her mother.

"Your daughter's very responsible," her mother notes.

"Yes," I say. "But she's not ready for a puppy."

Who ever is? A new puppy turns a household upside down. He bites everything. He relieves himself where he pleases. One afternoon, I wake from a nap to find him sleeping on my larynx.

"He needs to go out," I say.

"Why?"

"Trust me," I say. "He needs to go out."

Puppies are bred by a consortium of carpet salesmen and floor refinishers. They have damaged more oak than lightning and wind combined. When puppies aren't christening the floors, they are scoping out that new chair you just reupholstered or the carpeting in the bedroom. "Hey, this looks nice," the puppy thinks. "Textured Karastan. My favorite."

Then there's that breath of theirs, a combination of whiskey and truck exhaust. Hemingway had breath like that, most likely. With the faint traces of a bad cigar.

"Who's paying for his shots?" I ask.

"Shots?"

"Dogs cost more than children," I tell my daughter.

"Don't worry, Dad."

"Worry?" I ask. "Never."

Like many college kids, my daughter has not fully weighed the financial consequences of this new acquisition. It's much like the way they buy cars, thinking of only the sticker price and not the taxes, insurance, registration, delivery charges, gasoline, oil changes, and all the other ways a car costs you. I guess that's what dads are for. To think ahead. To ask questions.*

"Ever heard a beagle bark?" I ask my daughter.

"No."

"You're in for a treat."

Two days later, the beagle barks his first bark. It is the mournful wail of a man about to be beheaded. Each bark lasts five seconds. Then another one comes. He scares himself with his own noises, so he barks some more.

At eight weeks old, the dog is all bark and all bite.

"He chews everything," my older daughter says.

"He tickles," the little girl says, laughing.

"Ouch," says the boy, attacked by the pup's sewing-needle teeth. "Ouch-ouch-ouch."

The puppy's name is Koa. You know, like the campgrounds. My daughter explained that it is a Hawaiian word for something I can't quite remember. Probably campground.

Despite his youth and loopy demeanor, this puppy seems to be fairly bright. He thinks my wristwatch is his mother. Or he thinks I am his mother and my watchband is some sort of teat.

Then again, maybe he's not that bright. While playing with dust bunnies, which he assumes are alive, the puppy gets stuck beneath the armoire. A day or two earlier, he slid out easily on a belly as soft as cake. Now he's grown enough to get pinned in. He yelps. Stuck.

Meanwhile, our eight-year-old dog is eating the puppy's food. The puppy pops free and runs to eat the cat food. The cat eats the baby's food. And all I can think: *Wish we had gone with that Pergo flooring.*

"I think life was better," I tell my wife, "when our daughter was just trying to kill us with fancy desserts."

"And your point?" she asks.

"That things can always get worse," I tell her.

We are—more than usual even—a household in turmoil. My March Madness bracket is a disaster. The cars need work. School projects are behind schedule. No one has eaten a vegetable in, like, four days.

And on Saturday, a red-chested robin is in the garage eyeing the rafters for her nest. Lot of curb appeal, our house. There's the entire rest of the world, but this mother robin picks our place to start a family, up in the dry, dark pine rafters of the garage, where the hula hoops are stored. Who keeps hula hoops anymore? I guess we do.

And as I write this, a pregnant sparrow is tapping on a window that looks out over the ever-greener backyard, asking if we might spare a room.

"Believe me, pal," I warn her, "this is no place for living things."

Yet, they keep coming: puppies, toddlers, the pregnant birds—to the loud, little home under the olive trees. To the house with a hundred heartbeats.**

**The older daughter responds:**
*\* Don't be fooled by the thin veil of bitterness you hear throughout this entire recounting. My dad conveniently fails to leave out how he fell literally head over heels for Koa at first sight. I mean, he saw Koa in the front yard for the first time and took a full*

*toddler's tumble into the yard to be side by side, immediately spooning the dog and giggling at the puppy's licks that covered his face.*

*\*\* My dad and the 300-pound beagle were best pals from the start and, thirteen years later, their age has brought them even closer together as their biological clocks—from the snoring before even fully asleep, to the frequent bathroom trips at night, to the more restricted diets—have bonded them in a way my dad never saw coming.*

# DROPPING HER AT THE DORM

*August 29, 2009*

Our Pickett's Charge into the Midwest is a roaring success. We drop off the little girl at a fine school that, for a mere thirty or forty grand, will keep tabs on her for an entire academic year. Good deal, I say. Heck, she spends that much on Starbucks.

"I'd have paid more," I tell Posh.

"We don't have any more," she says.

"Oh."

By the way, if you're taking a daughter to college soon, might I recommend renting one of those C-130 transport planes, a whopping-big aircraft with abundant trunk space. That's what we did, and it took us only two round-trip flights.

The first load was entirely shoes. The second trip was scarves and scrapbooks. We shipped the rest ahead of time. (Thanks, UPS!)

Not since the Berlin Airlift has the world experienced anything like this. Evidently, freshman year now requires four tons of clothes, hangers, little clutch purses, cheap IKEA storage units, tape dispensers, tennis rackets, silverware, ramen noodles, gauze. I swear, Posh and I were married twenty years before we accumulated this much junk.

Still, the little girl forgot a few things. Here, in her words, is the email list of items she needs us to send:

☞ lavender body lotion that's by my sink

☞ hair products near the lamp on my dresser in the bathroom (pink

Bed Head bottle, clear shiny bottle with gray top)

☞ perfume (Anna Sui on my dresser)

☞ hanger clips, they are attached to my shoe rack in my closet

☞ one white shoe rack from on top of my closet

☞ scarf rings that are hanging from my closet

☞ your brown Uggs [meaning her mother's]

☞ safety pins

☞ Trader Joe's dried mango, trail mix, some Arizona iced tea, any other nice goodies you're willing to throw in . . .*

Hey, kid, how about me? I'm a "goodie." I'd be handy to have around the dorm for a few weeks. Dogs and dads. That's what a real home requires. And the smell of garlic from the kitchen. Not scarf rings. Not Anna Sui perfume.

As you can see, the little girl is a little too brand conscious sometimes, a California kid now living among the children of the corn. Our daughter prefers those big sunglasses that make her look like a bumblebee, and she spends too much on the coolest T-shirts and shorts.

Yeah, she's cool, all right. Wait till her classmates find out she still believes in Santa Claus.

Emotionally, the trip went fine. In an effort to keep us strong, I barely blubbered at all—at least publicly, which is a nice change for me.

I am, by nature, a "stablist," in the sense of wanting as much stability in life as possible and very little change. All that hooey you hear about change being good is just some MBA motivational tactic. Most change is rotten, and everybody knows it.

If it were up to me, our daughter would still be eight years old and the only time she would leave is for sleepovers at Amanda's house.

Now, she's at the ultimate sleepover, an American college. I'll never forget standing outside her un-air-conditioned dorm last week, staring up at this four-story cinderblock monstrosity, thinking, "We've really sent her here? Was she convicted of something?"

There were box fans in every single window, so many that I feared her dorm might actually lift from the ground, like that house in *Up*.

To keep the building earthbound, we filled it with stuff. Boxes. Suitcases. Our daughter.

When we finally got everything in, we stalled awhile to make sure she was settled. After the third day of this, we decided it was time to say goodbye. By then, I was pretty sure one of us might melt. Turns out I have a heart, for I think I heard it buzzing. Or maybe I inhaled a locust. All I know is that I couldn't speak.

So, so long, baby. Weather is certain to be a factor in your first semester there in the Middle West. First, the blistering heat. Then, the blistering cold.

In between, we hope, there will be one of those glorious Midwestern falls. The big campus is thick with oaks and maples, and they are bound to be aglow in early October. If it's an especially good year, maybe the trees will match the fire in the cheeks of you and your classmates, so fresh-faced and excited about this great escape.

Really, is there anything better than freshman year? I think not.

Back home, amid the click-click-click of the clock on the mantel—or your too quiet bedroom—I am working to remember that.

\* **Posh adds**:
*He forgot one thing that the college girl asked us to send: her little brother.*

**The columnist responds:**
*I would've been glad to.*

# POSH FALLS IN HER OWN PURSE

*September 26, 2009*

We're trying to avoid the "pig flu" that's sweeping the first grade—the little guy's term, not mine—so we're headed back to the heartland, of all places. Seems if you were wary of swine, this is the last place you'd ever want to go.

Anyway, that's where we are, at my daughter's college in Indiana—the land of crunchy sushi, a place where you can't get a decent martini to save your life.

"Anything for our kids," I explain.

"Evidently," says my wife.

Seems we just dropped off the little girl, yet we are back. "Parents' Weekend," they call it. We walk by one frat house, and there are empty Jell-O shot cups all over the lawn, like birch leaves. Obviously, the children are putting on their best fronts for Mom and Dad.

If you've never had a Jell-O shot, it is Jell-O mixed with vodka or some other rotgut alcohol. You pour it into tiny plastic cups, then chill it solid. Kids here really like their Jell-O. It's almost a food group.

"Did you see the bicycle in the tree this morning?" one of the little girl's classmates asks.

"Yeah, I saw it," someone answers.

No, I don't approve. If it were up to me, the drinking age here would be raised to fifty. By then, you've earned a snort or two and are too tired to do much damage, really. It's hard to imagine a fifty-year-old having too many Jell-O shots and deciding to park his Schwinn high up in some sugar maple.*

I think Posh would agree. She's not much for the sauce herself. She's one of those tiny wives with big purses who likes to maintain total focus at all times, except when she doesn't. In fact, on the way to the airport, she started digging for something and tumbled headfirst into her giant purse.**

After a few minutes, I decided to fish her out. (She had our boarding passes.) Unfortunately, she was the smallest thing in her purse. You know how it is—you look and look and look, knowing she's got to be in there somewhere. If she hadn't bit my thumb, I might never have found her.

So how's the little girl? Great, thanks. The California kid is loving the heartland and vice versa. She's made a litter of new buddies.

After a month, it is as if they've known one another for decades.

On Saturday, we all go to the football game together, the parents and the kids. The game's close, we lose, who cares? It's one of those crazy Big Ten games where the marching band is better than the football team and they flip the cheerleaders clear up into the clouds. I fear one or two might still be up there, circling the Earth—still smiling.

After the game, the kids cluster together on a hillside like kittens, while the parents get to know one another better over beer. Never tried the stuff before. I find it fizzy but refreshing.

As if that weren't enough, one dad brought lobster sandwiches all the way from New England. So I've got a lobster roll in my right claw and a cold beer in my left. If you've found a better way to spend an autumn afternoon—new friends, cold beer, and succulent lobster—please call. I'm pretty free the rest of my life.***

Best of all is seeing the kids so happy. Are these the same moody little monsters who drove us crazy through high school? Guess not. They already seem more poised, more patient, more everything.

At dinner, another California kid tells a wonderful story of arriving for freshman year. In the first week, the girl started seeing these flashes of light that worried her. She didn't know any classmates well enough to confide in them, so she went to the campus clinic, fearing the worst.

"Dear, you're from California, right?" the nurse asked.

"Yes."

"Um, have you ever seen fireflies before?"

"Fireflies?"

College: It's all about discovery.

In the end, Parents' Weekend turns out to be a blast. It's my favorite new holiday, after Mardi Gras and Bill Murray's birthday. Next year, the dads vow, we're going to rent an RV. We'll park it in a shady spot near the stadium, fire up a grill, rent our own mini-marching band, with ten snares and twenty trumpets, to serenade us. Some guys waste their money on personal jets. We prefer to support the arts.

Frankly, though, it'll be hard to top this year. We received lots of hugs from the little girl, who's never been shy that way. She is the huggiest kid you could ever want, assuming you ever wanted a huggy kid (some don't).

"Charlie has mono!" she squeals one morning after hearing that someone in their group fell sick.

"Oh?"

"I think," the little girl says, "that all my friends should be tested."

"Is that necessary?"

"Well, we all kiss each other."

"Huh!!!" blurted her mother, who proceeded to fall into her own purse for a second time.

Full gainer, with a perfect half twist. This time, we just let her rest.

**\* Posh responds:**
*The dads succeeded in out-drinking the kids year after year.*

**\*\* The columnist adds:**
*This is one of the columns readers remember most often, and it's because of the falling-into-her-own-purse stuff. I think it happens more than women want to admit.*

**\*\*\* Posh adds:**
*Good food, great company, and lots of hugs from the kids. Does it get any better?*

**The columnist answers:**
*No.*

# SO LONG, FIRST GRADE

*June 19, 2010*

Dear first graders,

At the end of the year, here are a few things I'd like to bring to your attention: You approach each day as if you've already had a glass of $100 champagne. Your entire lives have been like the second hour of a very good wedding reception.

As with champagne itself, you have lots of bubbles and none of them has been burst—Santa Claus, the Easter Bunny, corporate capitalism. They all thrive in your crazy, pudding-filled heads.

The other day, my own son—who is one of you—lifted his head to the sky and blew, thinking he could move the clouds.

First graders, huh? Get a grip, you kids.

Don't you know how life beats you down? Don't you know yet about the discrepancy between dreams and outcomes?

No, obviously you don't. You stand around each morning before class, talking about the teeth you lost overnight and noting how the new gaps in your smiles are great for milkshake straws. "My dad pulled out my tooth," Ava says. "He just grabbed it and twisted. There was blood."

Oh, quit your bragging, Ava.

I see you and your little buddies each day before class, waiting for Mrs. Patterson to open the classroom door, hungry for her great New York accent.* You soak it up with your pink-tipped ears, like baby mice. You are seven, and while you wait you wiggle like the inner workings of an old watch. You wear your heartbeats on your snotty little sleeves.

Listen, I've been studying you all year, and I have reached this disturbing conclusion: You have no apparent cliques, you kids. I mean, what are you thinking? This is LA, for gosh sakes, where we don't even let people into NBA games unless they make $1.5 million (a week).

I see what you're up to. You're weirdly egalitarian in a world that no longer celebrates such things. You mingle each day as if at some college mixer. Evidently, a first grader doesn't care much for fashion, or fancy haircuts, or what your daddy does. All a first grader cares about is whether you laugh at his silly jokes. Then you're in his frat. It is a very big frat—the biggest in the world. That doesn't mean it's the best.

Seriously, you're all nuts. You're showoffs, too. I've volunteered in the classroom several times over the course of the school year, helping you with your reading, only to discover some of you have larger vocabularies than I do.

So, not only are you excessively fair, you're scary smart. I think I hate you. You might be as perfect as people ever get.

On occasion, I also read to you. During Dr. Seuss Day, I read you a book with so many "whatcha-ma-jiggies" and "thinga-ma-bops" that I grew faint-headed and spilled out of my chair. You thought I was joking when I fell to the floor, not realizing that I am a man of substance. I never joke. When I give wedding toasts, for example, they are somber expressions about the dangers of commitment, like something Tolstoy would write after a stormy fling.

But back to the subject at hand: first graders. Don't care much for you guys. Never have. Never will.

One day, before a field trip, the entire class sang a few songs to get the day rolling. You sang a heartfelt "My Country, 'Tis of Thee," then a rousing "Take Me Out to the Ballgame." In one hundred years, schoolkids will still be singing 'My Country, 'Tis of Thee" and "Take Me Out to the Ballgame," a small and comforting realization in a large and ornery world.

Okay, I'll give you that. Occasionally, you can be kind of cute.

Before we forget, let's be sure to thank Mrs. Patterson for all she did. Teaching you knuckleheads to read, for example. Teaching you to focus, to organize, to function as part of a wild and disparate group.

Teaching you to write. Teaching you that *M*s are not rainbows and that each letter cannot be an entirely different size or color. When my little guy first began to write, the *O*s were quite large and the *B*s quite minuscule. He took pride in the variation. He worked hard to make each character unique.

Somehow, Mrs. Patterson straightened him out. As with the alphabet itself, she made him part of a group but let him be his own unique self.

Now, to thank her, you kids are leaving, heading off to second grade. In my experience, that's how kids show their appreciation. They leave. No one should ever take it personally.

So, goodbye, Mrs. Patterson; celebrate this moment. There must be a special corner of heaven for first-grade teachers. Sort of a VIP section, where the margaritas keep flowing and no one ever screams.

And goodbye, you first graders. Summer awaits, long and lazy— traditionally a bubble-rich environment.

Catch a ballgame. Lose some teeth. Move some clouds.

But don't you dare forget first grade, when you were as perfect as people ever get.

**\* The little guy responds:**
*She was the strictest teacher out there. But she was fun and gave us treats.*
*She also gave us fake dollars, which she called "Patterson Dollars."*
*Whoever earned the most got to take home one of the class animals.*

**The columnist adds:**
*Which is how we met his little friend Joey.*

# WITH MOM GONE, HOME'S JUST A HOUSE

*March 31, 2012*

The thing about my mother's eulogy is that I used note cards. After fifty-five years, you'd think you could remember a mother without such prompts. But this was no regular mother. Tell me, are there any regular mothers?

She could be hell in high heels, my mom—a little French, a little fussy about what other people wore on airplanes these days. She once bought a Christmas tree, hauled it home, decorated it with a thousand lights and a million ornaments, then took the whole thing down and returned it to the tree lot.

"It's not quite right," she told the puzzled tree man.

Hey, Mom, I said: That tree isn't the only thing that's "not quite right."

We'd visit her every summer on the outskirts of Chicago. It's not Anywhere USA, but close. Where farms once stood, now subdivisions. In what passes for progress, Walmarts have replaced wetlands.

My mother died peacefully in her sleep the other night on the same shady street where she was born in 1924. Who does that anymore? She was of another time. In summer, she'd fill big pickle jars with flowers from her yard and surprise neighbors with them. Who does that either?

We buried her on the first day of spring, in a dark blue casket she'd picked out herself. Picasso had what is known as his Blue Period. Lasted about three years. My mom's blue period lasted nine decades: blue furniture, blue garden, blue clothes.

And, finally, this blue coffin. A dozen years ago, she went down to the funeral home and selected it on her own, fearing that the rest of us would not share her same exquisite sense of style. When the sun hit it, my sister noted at the gravesite, it looked like a ski boat.

We buried her on the first day of spring, in the creamy Midwestern soil she loved so much. It was an uncommonly warm March morning, in the mid-eighties, just like her. In the backyard, a cherry tree had burst with blossoms overnight—spooky and divine all at once.

Neighbors came to the garden party after and spoke of how she'd inspired them and remembered that great laugh of hers, the loudest laugh in the room. Her mind was sharp till the very end. She mowed her own yard till she was almost eighty. She shoveled snow, cleaned the gutters, drove, lived alone, sipped her nightly bourbon.

If there's something for us to glean from all this, it's to stay crazy-active, to treat old age like a strong wind you face head-on. She never thought of herself as elderly, had no patience with self-pity. When she finally needed a pacemaker, I told the doctor to err on the safe side: "Give her three."

Life moved through her house like light through crystal. I remember the little things. Snow against the streetlight. The way the lawn smelled after mowing. The pink prairie sunsets. How, as kids, we would play all over the neighborhood from dawn to dusk on summer days—mosquito bites, sunburns, Bactine.

But mostly, this house has lost its hum.

We will sell it now, the place Mom and Dad built on the edge of town and raised two beautiful children in—plus me. My sisters and I are hopelessly sentimental about some things, but it becomes increasingly clear that she was this house, and without her, it's just another three-bedroom ranch with a big yard and gutters full of willow leaves.

So, no, there are no regular mothers. Just yours. Just mine. Most don't leave huge histories. They live on in the smiles of their grandchildren, and their children, and the children after that.

On the wall of her house, this poem:

> One hundred years from now, it will not matter what kind of car I drove, what kind of house I lived in, how much was in my bank account, nor what my clothes looked like.

> But the world may be a little better because I was important in the life of a child.

Thanks, Mom.

**The columnist adds:**
*This is another column folks refer to and remember fondly.*
*Pretty sure I did only one draft, and this is it. She was a force of nature, my mom.*

# TURNING SIXTY

*November 19, 2016*

Driving down into the city at dusk, into that rosy quilt of LA lights. Twinkle-twinkle, little town . . . how I wonder what I've found.

Feeling Raymond Chandler—obviously—feeling a little Leonard Cohen as well.

Going to miss Mr. Cohen, who died the other day. He had a wry humor and a belchy voice that seemed to come out of the back end of an old truck. A genius is what he was. I preferred his work over Dylan's.

Most everybody's favorite song-sonnet from the Cohen collection:

> Your faith was strong but you needed proof,
>
> You saw her bathing on the roof,
>
> Her beauty and the moonlight overthrew you.
>
> She tied you to a kitchen chair,
>
> She broke your throne, and she cut your hair,
>
> And from your lips she drew the Hallelujah.

I am a collector of wry lyrics, vintage cars, and rare children. Seemed a banner week for such things.

For instance, the old Camaro passed the smog test, a significant shocker. Vegas was giving ten to one that the car would fail the smog test—twenty-five to one that it would actually burst into flames—after which I'd be thumbing rides with an empty guitar case slung across my back. Drivers are attracted by that and quick to pull over: "Sure, I'll pick up that scruffy troubadour. Looks too old to be much trouble."

Which is true. Last week, I hit sixty, and I'm not much trouble, though for two months I've strung my buddy Bittner along, convincing him my birthday was more imminent than it actually was.

Bittner kept buying me drinks and picking up the tab for happy hour egg rolls and such. It was really something to watch, the way he bought in. Worked out so well, I think I'll have another birthday next month.*

But last week, I finally joined Club Sixty. Like my car, I make strange noises in the morning and my emissions are a little higher than they should be. Coming out of the shower the other day, I took a quick inventory in the steamy mirror. Shoulders? Strong. Stomach? Okay. Back end? Like an aging emu.

So, all in all, sixty seems okay. In lieu of a red Lamborghini, which is what I really needed, my two sons made me dinner to mark the occasion: rib eyes, asparagus gift-wrapped in bacon, macaroni salad. It was a feast fit for a deranged king—cooked perfectly, then cooked a little more, just the way I like it.

The boys' secret to searing steaks is to slap them on the grill, then watch the Lakers on TV till the fire department shows up. At that point, they know the steaks are almost done.

*Delicious* is too weak a word, not just for the beef but for the entire dining experience. We did pause at one point to tell the little guy that, when he fetches a dessert fork for himself, maybe he could fetch a dessert fork for everyone at the table. But instilling that sort of selflessness doesn't happen in one day, and we feel he's making great strides. Next week's lesson: How to hold the door for strangers. Coming soon: How to wash a water glass.

Later in the same week, my lovely and patient older daughter nearly one-upped her brothers with a surprise party at my favorite clangy saloon in Little Tokyo. Had I been ambushed by orangutans with machetes, I could not have been more surprised.

Twinkle-twinkle, little bar. . . . Not since the 1974 Oakland A's have we seen so many thirsty malcontents gathered in one small bar area. There were old friends, squirrely friends, tall ones, too. I almost feel a poem coming on, a Jimmy Stewart moment. I am as inspired by this festivus of funny friends as I am by my rare and generous children.

In sixty years, there are a few things I regret: Majoring in beer and pizza, for instance, was a bad idea—at least for me. Or betting fifty bucks on what turned out to be a purple unicorn at the recent Breeders' Cup.

Betrothing that Camaro turned out to be kind of a life mistake, as is expecting an angry, jam-packed metropolis like this to ever be the kind of rustic retreat I actually prefer.

But I sure never regret these four kids, who twinkle and glow a little more with each passing moon.

"Why me?" I sometimes ask a sky full of stars. "How did I get so lucky?" Hallelujah.

### * Bittner responds:

*The best part about celebrating the big six-oh with Chris was that, a week earlier, I had appropriated a credit card from our attorney, Billable Bob, while Bob was schmoozing a potential client. It was amazing how many new friends I made during that glorious period of time. Somehow Billable Bob got tipped off and immediately threw his legal prowess around to get the charges reversed. I am pretty sure that he knew that I had something to do with it. But to Bob's credit, he never mentioned a thing.*

### The columnist adds:

*I'm sure he billed you for his time. We don't call him Billable Bob for nothing.*

# HOLIDAYS

# HALLOWEEN IS HERE SOMEWHERE

*October 21, 2004*

Inside the house, there are fireplaces to clean and a door that needs to be reset. But hold on. The holidays beckon. Time to Halloween the front porch.

"What are you doing, Dad?"

"Halloweening the house," I explain.

The little girl stands on the porch watching me. She is like a letter waiting for a stamp. Nothing seems able to move her. The little girl is no doubt paralyzed by her admiration for me, her father, a man of action and vision, in a suburb starved for such things. Poor kid, stuck here on the front porch, postage due.*

"Here, grab this box," I say.

"Okay, Dad," she says, hugging it like a grandpa.

One by one, we bring the boxes up from the little half basement on the west side of the house. Most California homes don't have basements, an oversight, I guess, in the building craze of the twentieth century. Too bad, whatever the reason, for a basement is a man's land.

"I know there's another box down there," my wife says.

"Where?" I say.

"Somewhere," she insists.

Carefully, after every Halloween, I store away the decorations in boxes I snatch from behind the florist shop. They smell of roses and carnations and other near-dead things. I take them anyway. With free boxes, you can't be too choosy.

"I know there's another box," my wife says.**

And each year, when I bring them back out to decorate, my wife insists that one is missing. Always, there's another box that I can't find, even though I label them carefully, with the giant Magic Marker.
HALLOWEEN COSTUMES. HALLOWEEN PLATES AND DISHES

A few years ago, I gave up big cigars for giant Magic Markers, and have regretted it almost daily ever since.

"You should store them all together," she says.

"Now you tell me," I say.

"There's one box with tall things in it," she says, as if I have X-ray eyes.

With decorations, it always goes like this. It's worse at Christmas, but still the spousal pressure is relentless. I will spend twenty minutes looking for the missing box, then declare it stolen or swept away by flood, the explanation varies each year. In my view, it's a few well-chosen little lies that really keep a marriage going.

"You're not putting that up, are you?" she asks as I staple a cardboard vampire to a front-porch post.

"Of course not," I say, popping it in the forehead with another staple.

In truth, I am putting everything up. My wife, when she decorates, always leaves leftovers in a box, deeming some items worthy and others as too tired or tattered. I hang it all. I think it's less elitist that way. More of the America we used to know.

I tear down real spiderwebs and put up fake ones. I unfold vampires and witches first used fifteen years ago. Almost all of my Halloween decorations are either cardboard or plastic, the two mediums I prefer to work in. It's an aesthetic you don't see much outside the design centers of Paris or New York. But here you do—on a porch, in a suburb like any other.

With three thwacks of the staple gun, I hang a Frankenstein. With three deep breaths, I inflate a plastic pumpkin.

"Is that a giant orange?" the boy asks.

"Yes," I say.

"No, it's a pumpkin," the little girl says.

"Sure, go and ruin it for him," I say.

I explain to them that with my Halloween displays, everyone takes away something different. It's what sets it apart as true art.***

"In reality, everything's a little abstract," I explain.

"Sure, Dad," they say, then one by one filter off to their email or their cellphones, probably to brag to friends how fortunate they are.

"Can he play out here?" my wife says, setting the baby down on the porch.

"Why not," I say.

Unlike my wife, the baby blows kisses to me as I work. Everywhere he goes lately, the baby blows kisses to people. To grandmas at the grocery store. To the big Latino guy making crepes at the farmers' market.

Of course, by throwing kisses around like that, he is diminishing their very value. But you try explaining economics to a twenty-two-month-old who loves the world.

"How's this look?" I ask him as the porch fills with Halloween.

The baby sits on the porch watching me, him and that ever-present cocker spaniel, the world's first metrosexual dog.**** I love the dog, but he is obsessed with the luster of his own coat and skin, which he licks over and over again, like an actor preparing for a major part.

"You're clean now," I tell the dog. "Too clean."

"What about me?" the baby asks.

"You? Never," I say.

Out across the lawn, the birch tree is turning. In the north breeze, a certain chill.

And on the porch, the baby and the dog blink at me gratefully in the autumn sun. Happy for Halloween. Happy for little homegrown truths.

**The daughter adds:**
*\* Ha, how things have changed!*

*\*\* Literally, this is an argument they have every holiday, every year.*

*\*\*\* This little scene completely defines my dad's perspective on life. Where we see trashy junk, he sees true art.*

*\*\*\*\* To be fair, the dog's sexuality has never been established. He was a product of his environment.*

# A LITTLE CHURCH, A LITTLE CHILI

*December 30, 2004*

The full moon is coming up over the mountains like a big bowl of milk, and friends and neighbors are all entering church for Christmas Eve services. As the baby sits on my lap, I try to re-crease his cotton collar with my thumb and forefinger. Lots of luck.

"You look good in church," I tell him.

"Who doesn't?" he answers.

Of course, everybody looks good in church. The soft light. The stained glass. If I owned a nightclub, I'd copy this flattering look, invite the masses and collect my fortune.

"Please reach into your pocket . . ." the pastor says.

"Already?" I think to myself.

"And pull out your keys . . ." he says.

"Great, now they want my car," I tell my wife.

"Nobody would want your car," she whispers.

"And shake your keys as we all sing 'Jingle Bells,'" the pastor urges.

Hundreds strong, we rise to sing "Jingle Bells." Admittedly, I never really believed in the concept of a one-horse open sleigh. To pull a sleigh properly, you need at least two horses, young and strong. But I play along. It's Christmas.

Bells on bob-tail ring, making spirits bright,
What fun it is to ride and sing a sleighing song tonight . . .

I carry the congregation in song for a while, till I get short of breath, then just lip-synch. In my arms, the baby is jingling his older sister's car keys. A little cylinder of Mace, attached to the key chain, dangles in front of my eyes.

It occurs to me that this could easily turn out to be a very memorable Christmas Eve: the one when I got Maced in church.

We are a Catholic-Lutheran-Presbyterian-Irish-Italian-Ukrainian clan, with a splash of German blood thrown on top, like vermouth.

Belonging to this many factions—at one time or another—is a little like having too many credit cards in your wallet. For now, though, we have settled on this beautiful Presbyterian church. On Christmas Eve, it offers five services.

"Which service?" my wife asked earlier in the day.

"The Packers won't be done till three," I warned.

"We'll go at four," she said with a sigh.

Tone-deaf but loud, I now sit on the end of the row so as not to poison the beautiful carols. I seem to be surrounded by well-dressed men who always seem to have $100 bills in their pockets.

How liberating that must be to always have an extra hundred handy for a good haircut or a round of golf. I make a mental note to work harder next year.

"This is such a nice church," says a visitor.

"We really like it," I say.

The Christmas Eve service moves swiftly. It is mostly music, mostly performed by kids. It is a party atmosphere, free of guilt, blame, shame, abashment, and other wicked tools some faiths seem to rely upon.

Gentle as lambs, we end one portion of the service by singing happy birthday, dear Jesus. Happy birthday to you.

Like you, I could do without all the holiday hype. The overspending. The traffic. But Lord I love Christmas Eve. The best buzz in town.

Speaking of alcohol, I remember my father putting together toys for my younger sisters, the tremble in his fingers that urbane men get when they try to do something with their hands.

He could pour a martini without a flinch, but you'd dread the moment he picked up a screwdriver. Big Irish face, like Charles Durning, down on the carpet grunting and cursing the poor saps who wrote the directions.*

As a kid, I remember friends coming by. The phone ringing. Dogs jumping at the door. To this day, I believe a good Christmas Eve is part magic, part turmoil.

So at home later, my wife and I have a few co-workers over to tip a glass and enjoy chili and turmoil.

Oh, and of course Christmas tamales. With a spoon of chili over them, tamales are among our finer local delicacies and one of the best meals you can find. Outside of a ballpark, anyway.

"I wonder if they eat chili in Chile," someone wonders, giving you a sample of the level of our party rhetoric.

"Anybody seen *Spanglish?*" I ask. "Anybody?"

"I'm still looking for one person who's seen *Joey*," my buddy Tom says. "Just one person."

As is usually the case, Christmas Eve goes by too quickly. Good song. Spicy food. Fast company. At one point, the baby drops his trousers and parades around the living room, clucking like a duck and hugging people he barely knows. His eyes collect the candlelight. Everybody laughs.

"How much did he drink?" I ask my wife.

"Have you seen the cat?" she asks.

Cluck-cluck, the baby says, then smooches my buddy Vic hard on the lips. Last spotted, the baby was shimmying up the Christmas tree, hunting for grouse.

Each December, we hurl ourselves at Christmas, wagering that God has a sense of humor . . . a wry eye . . . a tolerance for human foible.

Lord help us if we're wrong.

**\* The columnist adds:**

*My dad loved Christmas Eve, too, so maybe I got it from him, this love of the holidays. Mom was kind of a junkie also, though. I was doomed from the outset. There are a healthy number of Christmas columns in this collection—maybe too many. It's just such a colossal mess of a holiday. Definitely our best holiday.*

# CUPID STRIKES AGAIN

*February 12, 2003*

"Hey, Pops, got any money in that wallet?"

He's a teenager now, alternately charming and insane. When he wants money, he's charming. When I won't let him do something, he's insane. Don't worry, they grow out of it.

"Yep, I bet there's money in there," the boy says with a wink.

Now, the boy has done nothing to deserve money, other than to sleep till noon and eat half the refrigerator. Not just the food. The refrigerator, too.

The sandwich I saved from last night? Gone. Half a gallon of ice cream? Melts in his mouth.

"Come on, Dad, I need money for Valentine's," he moans.*

"Who for?"

"Who do you think?"

"Her?"

"Yeah, her," he says.

I discover later that there are a lot of "hers" in the world. I assumed "her" was still his mother. Turns out, "her" is someone else. Of all the advice I will ever give you, remember this one: Beware of pronouns.

"He bought that for you?" I ask later about a gift on the dining table.

"You kidding?" his mom says. "It was for her."

I smell of two things, baby spit and yard work. Just in time for Valentine's.**

"Could you maybe change your T-shirt?" my wife asks.

The musk of a parent's life isn't just in the clothes. It's in the furniture. In the walls. In the skin. You young kids remember that in the back seat on Friday nights. Parenthood has a scent that doesn't wash out.

"It's not the shirt," I tell my wife.

On TV, the news anchor is wearing a pink dress, another sign of Valentine's Day. During commercial breaks, a store advertises diamond necklaces at low monthly payments.

If I felt better about our relationship, I might invest in the necklace. But four hungry kids. A needy dog. A cat that is either asleep or dead. That's no future. That's a Johnny Cash song.

With my luck, I'll be left with two years of $14.99 payments and nothing.

"Hey, hand me that burp rag," my wife coos.

The baby is now her obsession. Frankly, I don't understand it. Sure, his skin is like linen. His eyes as bright as a winter sunrise. But his butt is all diaper. He constantly spits up. He has no visible means of support. All in all, he's me twenty years ago, fresh from college.

"Dad, are you jealous of the baby?" the little girl asks.

"No way."

"You're jealous of the baby," the little girl announces.

A little jealousy never hurt a relationship. In fact, it can invigorate it.

So I will try to win back my wife's affection. My first instinct? Get her drunk.

"Glass of wine?" I ask.

"I'm nursing," she says.

"So am I!"

"Go change your shirt," she says.

Off we go, the baby and I, shopping for Valentine's Day. "It's the thought that counts," I advise him. "But it'd better be an expensive thought."

He looks at me like I'm crazy. Romance today, it's beyond belief.

"Women are very aware of price," I tell him. "They'll know exactly what you paid."

"Just by looking at it?" he wonders.

"These women, they're like calculators," I say.

We browse the bath soaps. We consider concert tickets. Jewelry. Clothes. Cars. Plane tickets. Electronics. Stocks. Bonds. Pork bellies.

"What do you get the woman who has us?" I ask.

He cries at the thought.

"Imagine how she feels," I tell him.

Lingerie. Ice skates. Puppies. Goldfish. Encyclopedias.

"She has all these things," I finally tell him.

"She has everything," the baby says.

"And us," I say.

So the baby and I sit at a Starbucks, the way Robert Frost once did, and put down this poem:

*Roses are red, Dodgers are blue,*
*We went out gift shopping,*
*And found nothing, boo-hoo,*
*But we wrote down these words,*
*They're especially for you,*
*Our gift is our song, like Elton John used to.*
*So look in the driveway,*
*Glance under the bed,*
*You'll find only us,*
*Two guys with thick heads.*

"That's beautiful," the little girl says later.

"Thanks," I say.

Happy Valentine's.

**The older son adds:**

*\* I still need money for Valentine's Day!*

*\*\* He still smells like one of those things.*

**The columnist responds:**

*He's always been the funniest kid.*

# WILD PHEASANT ON A FORK

*December 19, 2009*

There are a few things I still like about the holidays. I like the way store clerks ask "credit or debit?"—words you can warm your hands by. I like the way Ann-Margret looks in *The Santa Clause 3*.

I like crows against low gray clouds . . . the first whiff of Fraser firs . . . wild pheasant on a fork.

I like that thick bacon you get from Niman Ranch. And the red velvet cakes at Porto's in Glendale, which is to bakeries what O'Hare is to air travel.

I like an open bar (big surprise). I like martini glasses against holiday lights and barkeeps in plaid bow ties.

I like how, when you open an old treasured book, the binding crackles like a log fire.

I like the kettle drum sounds kids make when they run on old wooden floors. I like the way Scotch tape sticks to their socks.

"It's a honey of a holiday!" sing the first graders in their Thursday morning recital.

Yeah, we'll see.

We're driving to young Colin's birthday party the other day. Colin is turning six, so it's a pretty big deal. Is it just me, or do half of all birthdays happen in December? I count back nine months and decide that March must be a very fertile time.

Anyway, we're driving to Colin's birthday party in that indeterminate part of the San Gabriel Valley—might be Arcadia, might be Temple City—when the little guy spots something out the window.

"Look at all those birds," he says. "What do you call it when they go places?"

"Migrating," I say.

"Vibrating?" he asks.

"Migrating."

"Look!" he says. "They just stopped to pick up some people!"

Like Santa, the little guy seems to see miracles that no one else sees. He spots something, and his eyes glisten like the crystal of a watch. I worry, sometimes, that he might grow up to be a writer.

But it's a week till Christmas, no time to be so negative. In fact, there are plenty of things to be excited about. For one, I finally got the outside lights up. Score!

When Posh complains about the delay, I tell her how I was tired of the same old lights on the same old house. She suggests I move.

Which brings up the usual whispered discussion of relationships and marriage in general, including such topics as:

☞ boredom

☞ lust

☞ division of duties

☞ harmless flirtations at holiday gatherings

☞ where the dog should sleep

☞ the creepy way I talk to inanimate objects (printers, remote controls, boats)

☞ the slobby way I dress around the house—"like Garth Brooks when he's cleaning out the garage," she says.

The hooded sweatshirt, I explain, is timeless and elegant—the black tux of the American suburb.

Then she brings up the incident where I almost punched an irritating know-it-all at a recent Christmas party.

"I don't look back, only forward," I tell her.

"But you wanted to punch him," she insists.

"Who?"

"Oh, never mind."

If I can continue to hold my punches, this is going to be one honey of a holiday.

I like board games on Christmas Eve. I like the way snow looks in old black-and-white movies.

I like ski racks on Porsches of a certain age . . . beat-up old toboggans . . . snow shoes from 1930.

I like slow-dancing a Christmas tree into the house. A little left. No, right. Okay, back a little. There.

I like stirring the chili, the gumbo, the soup and adding too much oregano and pepper.

I like pancakes and coffee on cold winter mornings.

I like wreaths on the fronts of buses.

Most of all, I like all those vibrating birds.

So the little girl arrives home today, her undergraduate career already one-eighth over. Lesson No. 1 you learn in college: All the good things in life go by far too fast.

We've been trying to make the house special for her, but not too special; otherwise, she would think she's in the wrong place and immediately turn around and leave.

Posh puts garland around the fireplace.

The little guy decorates the dog.

In that same spirit, I suggest pinning angel wings to Posh's back, a gesture that would reflect our true feelings about her. Jimmy Stewart's guardian angel gets wings. Why not mine?

But Posh passes on the angel wings, fearful that I might get carried away and start to paw her in front of strangers, which happens a lot with angels during the holidays.

Here's the deal: It won't take much to make the little girl feel at home again.

At Thanksgiving, she merely stood in front of the open refrigerator and—after three months of dorm food—made squeaky sounds of delight at the bounty that lay before her. Then she mewed.

She sounded to me like a small forest creature from a Burl Ives cartoon.

And, for a moment, I think she actually was.

Welcome home, squeaky. Merry Christmas to us all.

# CELEBRATING NOVEMBERFEST

*November 13, 2010*

With Novemberfest now upon us, I'd like to remind you that you cannot bring food into our house without someone lunging for it: a sandwich, a blintz, a side of pork. What usually happens is you'll be sitting there reading the paper—contentedly mumbling to yourself the way semi-sane people do—and someone will stroll by and just take a huge bite of whatever you're eating.

Particularly vulnerable are the Bay Cities sandwiches (on Lincoln in Santa Monica). Los Angeles is not really a great sandwich town, so when the lovely and patient older daughter brings by a gloppy Bay Cities sub, it's like the first day of deer season in Duluth.

Seriously, I've seen fistfights.

With that warning in mind, we barrel head-on toward Thanksgiving, the gloppiest holiday of the year.

At our house, we celebrate the Armenian Thanksgiving, which comes a little later than the traditional Thanksgiving—twelve days or so—or maybe I'm thinking of Christmas. My wife, Posh, dresses up as Cher for both occasions, which always throws people off. She also dresses like Cher for Mother's Day at church, which has doubled attendance among her fellow Presbyterians.

Cher and Cher alike, I always say.

In any case, it's a festive time, this Novemberfest. There are turkeys in the supermarket, and Armstrong already has trees strung with holiday lights. Thanks to all the rain, it's been a particularly lush fall—the hillsides poker-table green and the trees all ruddy in the cheeks.

Inspired by all of this, the little guy and I have been running through his lines for the Pilgrim pageant, which takes place soon. His teacher, Mrs. Norris, is considered sort of the Spielberg of second-grade plays. I wouldn't be surprised if she gets a deal with HBO soon, maybe to develop the next *Sopranos*.

The tagline: "The mob may be scary, but second grade is scarier."

So, anyway, everybody is expecting joy and insight from the second-grade Thanksgiving Pageant. It's our little suburb's version of a Lakers game.

This year's performance is titled "Popcorn! Popcorn! Popcorn!" You might guess that it involves popcorn, but there is so much more—allegory, deft characterization, subtext, surprise.

As I understand it, the play involves a bunch of Pilgrim kids going off to the multiplex, which gives them the opportunity to talk about popcorn.

"Mmmm! This popcorn is so tasty!" the little guy's character says. "It's crunchy and munchy too! And best of all, popcorn is good for you!"

You should hear the seven-year-old rehearsing the line. He's physical in that same way Brando was, tossing things and clenching his fists, and you're never quite sure what he's going to say next. Usually, it's "Um, Dad, I forgot the next line," at which point I remind him of his next line, and off he goes again.

At one point, the little guy has to say: "The Incas used popcorn for jewelry. Scientists found corn in a cave in New Mexico. The scientists think the corn is about 4,000 years old. Even the Indians who first saw Christopher Columbus ate popcorn."

I don't know how historically accurate this is, but I have often given popcorn as jewelry. Posh wears it with a little black dress on those nights when she really wants to feel good about herself and get people talking.

"Maybe you should try hanging a slice of salami from your ears," I've suggested in the past.

"That would be overkill," she sniffs.

What a prude.

Seriously, can you imagine going in for a little nuzzle and seeing a nice slice of Milanese salami dangling like an earring? I think I'm speaking for every husband when I say that women's fashion really should incorporate more junk food.

Ladies, dangle a nice cheese blintz around your neck, then see if your love life doesn't just take off.

After all, it's all about appearing good enough to eat, and who really has time for three meals a day anyway? At our house, we pretty much just chow down spontaneously on anything within range (see Bay Cities above).

In "Popcorn! Popcorn! Popcorn!" they don't really explore this food-as-fashion issue in as much depth as you'd like in a holiday classic. The play is more focused than that, which is why (I think) it might be up for a Pulitzer.

"Wow! Popcorn is so interesting," one of the kids says toward the end.

It really depends how you wear it.

# A MERRY LITTLE CHRISTMAS?
# GOOD LUCK

*December 20, 2008*

It's not even Christmas yet, and I've already gained five pounds, most of it on my face. Five pounds doesn't sound like a lot, unless it's all in your jowls. Besides, I have been gaining five pounds every Christmas for about twenty years now, which adds up to one hundred pounds in my face alone. Christmas in your face. Is there any other way?

Meanwhile, round and round the parking garage I go, like John the Baptist, looking for a place to park. As with so many of the saints, I spot things in the future that no one else really sees. So when the brake lights of a Lexus turn crimson, I am waiting patiently for the eternity it takes the driver to actually back out.

I like a lot about an American Christmas. I like the way the kitchen windows steam when there's a roast in the oven. I like the way Nat King Cole croons, "Dressed up like Esk-EEE-mos . . ." I even like the smiling polar bears on a twelve-pack of Coca-Cola and the way Amy Grant looks in a sweater.

But most of all, I like getting a parking space within a mile of the mall entrance.

Into the mall we go, two of the kids and I, looking for a more sensible holiday. For all the obvious reasons, this is supposed to be a smaller Christmas, a more spiritual, reasonable Christmas, a retro celebration in which we return to basics.

Fat (fa-la-la-la) chance. The mall looks like a Trump wedding, or the ascension of an Egyptian king. This is what Christmas would look like if Bethlehem had been located on the Vegas Strip.

Oh, the zoomanity.

Yet, despite the crush, the chaos, we need a little Christmas, right this very minute.

The kids and I hurry into Barneys New York—a $199 T-shirt?—then scramble to the Martin & Osa next door—yes, a $39 blouse!

We dance *The Nutcracker* through Anthropologie, then stutter-step like Kobe Bryant into the humongous Barnes & Noble, which is crammed with folks who look like they're buying their very first book (at age forty).

I promise you, dear God, let me out of this place alive and I will never come to another mall again. I'll never make any more jokes about the way you designed giraffes or question any of your strangest decisions—like giving Tyra Banks her own show.

Just let me escape this insane parking garage with my two kids, ease out onto the busy boulevard, and creep contentedly and safely to my modest fortress in the foothills. In return, I will lead a more virtuous life, drop a fiver in the charity kettle, even cry at Karen Carpenter songs.

Please let me out of this place—where Christmas is measured in megapixels and $500 purses.

Lord, we need a little Christmas. Right this very minute.

I'll never forget the moment we arrived in California. We crossed the state line, and a sign said:

WELCOME TO CALIFORNIA (CLOTHING OPTIONAL)

I knew right then we'd picked an excellent place to raise a family.* I knew right then we'd have some very memorable holidays.

Eighteen years later, we are still happy with our decision, particularly during the holidays. We buy Christmas trees from Oregon, sweaters from Bangladesh, bourbon from Kentucky.

I don't know that I've ever bought anything made in California for Christmas, except for the insanely wonderful stories that fill our TV screens this time of year.

To me, the glory of Christmas can always be found in one of those snow globes of hope and humor that Frank Capra crafted, or from the wry and knowing stories of Jean Shepherd or Charles Schulz.

Idealistic? You bet. Cornball? Give me a double scoop. Hollywood has always had a knack for poking fun at our ridiculous expectations and finding a message in the mayhem. They don't call it Tinsel Town for nothing.

Can you even imagine Christmas without a young George Bailey riding a coal shovel across an icy pond, or Chevy Chase putting a staple through the outdoor lights? How about the way Judy Garland's eyes glisten in *Meet Me in St. Louis*—like ice rinks—or Will Ferrell stepping onto an escalator for the first time in *Elf?***

Hollywood is Santa. Its sleigh is brimming with national treasures. Even money-lovin' Hollywood, which gets so much wrong, at least gets Christmas right.

Why can't we?

"Dear Jesus, I hope you had a good Halloween," the little guy says during Sunday grace.***

He is completely serious. His sisters and big brother laugh so hard, they nearly fall off their thrones. His mom can't even keep a straight face. That's how grace goes lately—full of inadvertent one-liners.

The other night, we passed the hospital where the little guy was born nearly six years ago to the day.

"Hey, that's where you were born," I tell him.

"Hmm," he says.

"What's wrong?"

"I wonder if they miss me," he says.

For our family, Christmas is like a genetic defect. We celebrate it too hard, with too many expectations. You get a hint of this by the obsessive way we pick out a tree.

"I like this one," the little guy says.

"That's a fire hydrant," I say.

"How 'bout this one?" says the little girl.

"Can you spin it around?" my wife asks the attendant.

"Are you taking it dancing?" I ask.

"Dad, let's go to that other lot," the little girl suggests.

Da Vinci never cared this much about shape and form. Rembrandt never cared this much for color. Beethoven spent less time on a symphony than we do picking out a simple six-foot fire hazard.

Our budget for the perfect tree is $60, but Posh spots one for $89 that she kind of adores.

"Can we eat it for Christmas dinner?" I ask.

"No."

"Then we're not spending $89 on a tree," I say.

When we get the $89 tree home, it turns out to be mounted poorly and doesn't sit straight up in the stand (an extra seven bucks). At first, we bend it back straight, but once we get the 120 strings of lights and 48,000 ornaments on it, it begins to teeter again. A friend dubbed it the Leaning Tower of Christmas.

None of us has the energy or the time to de-decorate the tree, re-cut the trunk, buy another stand, then decorate the tree again (estimated time: twelve to fourteen hours).

So we've started a pool on when exactly it will fall over.

The smart money? Christmas Eve.

*Dear Santa,*

*Won't keep you long. You can cancel that Porsche I ordered earlier. Personal bankruptcy looms like one of Dickens' ghosts. I don't fear unemployment so much as I fear daytime television. That would very well do me in.*

*And I guess my request for peace on Earth will have to wait another year, too—there's no telling what those cowards with automatic rifles will try next.*

*So here, with a smaller and more-contented holiday in mind, is my revised Christmas list:*

• *A giant aspirin, as big as a hockey puck.*

• *Two hours Christmas Day to watch the Lakers crush the Celtics.*

• *One honest moment.*

*And if you can't manage the other two, I'll settle for the one honest moment, where I have the courage to tell the ones I love how truly crazy I am for them. I am head-over-heels nuts for my wife, my mom, my kids, and even my sisters (seriously).*

*Why I can't be more upfront about this is anyone's guess. It might be because I'm a dad. It might be because I'm originally from the Midwest. It might just be because I'm a notorious goof-up.*

*But if you can give me one honest moment over the holidays—maybe two—I'll tell them all how I feel about them, not to mention a few old friends whom I'm pretty loopy for as well.*

*Sappy? As a Fraser fir. Sensible? As a Sears sweater.*

*Welcome to California, Santa. Remember, clothing optional.*

## The columnist adds:

*\* For a writer, wry and dry are always good. This is exactly the feeling I got when we crossed the state line and saw a slob in a T-shirt with the f-bomb printed across the front.*

*\*\* Much of Hollywood's best work involves the holidays, including one of the most-perfect movies ever:* It's a Wonderful Life.

*\*\*\* Swear to God . . .*

# A SPLASHY FATHER'S DAY

*June 16, 2012*

Erma Bombeck, who had a pretty good way with words, once noted of her father:

"He opened the jar of pickles when no one else could. He was the only one in the house who wasn't afraid to go into the basement by himself. He cut himself shaving, but no one kissed it or got excited about it. It was understood when it rained, he got the car and brought it around to the door. When anyone was sick, he went out to get the prescription filled. He took lots of pictures . . . but he was never in them."

Don't know how I'll be remembered, but I hope it is with that kind of fondness, the selfless guy who took lots of pictures but was never in them. Perfect.

Took the daughters surfing the other day. I've noticed lately that most of the activities they like have dollar signs in front of them. In fact, one of them just legally changed her name to Vi$a. Tough decision. It was either that or Cha-Ching.

The place we went surfing was Santa Monica. You may have heard of it. It is famous in my mind for the little Mexican joint on Main Street that serves a $9 burrito that could easily feed China. There is also some sort of pier.

Santa Monica is also where the Coolest Guy Ever keeps an office. For $37, Matt Rosas of Malibu Longboards gives you a surf lesson, a wet suit and a very buoyant surfboard. Perfect.*

Matt belongs to that significant subculture of surf instructors, yoga teachers, and tennis pros who have devoted their lives to making us fit. I have never met one who wasn't thrilled in his or her line of work. While the rest of us wear hard shoes and throttle cellphones, they wear flip-flops, straw hats, and sunscreen. After penguins, they may be Earth's happiest inhabitants.

The Coolest Guy Ever starts our lesson up on the sand, where he teaches us how to paddle, where to position ourselves, where to put our hands when we push up to stand.

What makes him the Coolest Guy Ever is that he tells you just the right amount of stuff and is so relaxed that he makes me relaxed, which is hard to accomplish. I'm usually as tight as J.Lo's G-string.

Anyway, out on the water, my daughter Vi$a goes first, stands up. The lovely and patient older daughter goes next, stands up.

Turns out Vi$a is the best surfer of the three of us. The lovely and patient older daughter is also a very adept surfer, especially if you measure such things by decibels. During the lesson, she shrieks so loudly that it begins to interfere with the sonar of dolphins and submarines. At one point, I look over to see the US Navy asking her to keep it down a little.

Me, I do okay. At this point in my life, I'm made mostly of jelly dough-nuts. You know how the Japanese feed beer to Kobe cattle? That's the dietary principle I follow: that if you eat and drink delicious things, you will become a more appealing and delicious person.

The other day, I had this argument with my wife over nutrition. She argued for the organic brand of peanut butter (which she buys), and I argued for the purchase of some Skippy (the kind that tastes good).

"Okay, when you die ten years too early . . . " she starts to say at one point.

"It'll be with a big smile on my face," I say, finishing her sentence.

This day, I also have a big smile on my face because, for the first time in my life, I am standing up on a surfboard. Not elegantly. Not with any sense of cool or control.

I find surfing especially challenging since what they call my "core muscle group" isn't a complete group; it's more like a single tendon, or maybe a sock.

But, thanks to the Coolest Guy Ever, I am actually surfing. One daughter and I even manage a tandem ride on the same board.

"Hey, Vi$a, lift me over your head!" I yell to her, and she immediately doesn't.

Surfing. What a buzzy way to start a summer. What a buzzy way to put sunbeams in your children's smiles.

Yes, I took lots of pictures.

Happy Father's Day.

**\* The older daughter responds:**

*This was a particularly fun Father's Day because, for once, my dad didn't just want peace on Earth. So, we went on an adventure. As the three eldest children have grown older, my father has become increasingly fond of finding fun activities to do together, and this one was a "splash" of a time, as he put it. We will remember every spill and dolphin shriek forever. We probably haven't been surfing since . . . but who can beat that company?*

# FINALLY, A PERFECT FAMILY CHRISTMAS

*January 10, 2015*

There's this coffee cup I like. It's chipped, but in a spot on the rim that would never touch your lips. When dirty, I put it in the dishwasher. When clean, I nudge it back on the shelf. At some point, one of the children—livid over some unrelated thing—will spot the flawed cup and slam it in the trash, thinking it's past its prime.

Till then, I cherish the little coffee cup with the chipped lip. It seems to have lived a little. It's not stained or otherwise unpleasant, but that little imperfection makes it stand out from all the other coffee cups. Like Marilyn Monroe's mole.

There's this house I like. Our house. Like the coffee cup, it has chips in spots that never touch your lips. There are cobwebs in the eaves, even after the winter rains, and it could use a coat of paint and a pair of shutters and some geraniums in a window box. But it seems to have lived a little. Like photos of rainy Paris streets, something about this house makes you want to go inside.

We cleaned it of Christmas the other day, though not completely. As is tradition, there is always some little remnant that doesn't get boxed up. This is not on purpose. You can scour the place, go over it seventeen times, and there will always be a Santa serving spoon or an ornament you discover a week later under the couch.

Knowing this, I tried to talk my wife into letting me use the leaf blower to de-Christmas the house, to start at one end and—as gardeners do—bazooka the tinsel, tree needles, slipper fuzz, cracker crumbs, twist ties, broken baby Jesuses, half-dead candles, chestnut husks, North Pole swizzle sticks, and the holiday cards everybody worked so hard on. In twenty seconds, I could leaf-blast it all right out of the house and into the neighbor's yard.*

There. Done. Ho-ho-ha!

That's often my way of solving problems, turning them into worse problems, but I do it with such spectacle and showmanship that for a moment you don't even care.

It's that way with Christmas. If it's a little broken, I can usually make it so much worse.

Not this year. Ours was, in fact, an amazing Christmas.

Usually sarcastic, droll, moody, edgy, and taking inventory of every little slight, our four kids were remarkable this year. I can't help but think they were pranking me, or that Posh drugged them or brought in impostor children to portray them over a couple of days.

In any event, it worked.

Patient and appreciative, the kids wowed me with their cheery holiday chutzpah. They even accompanied me on a long walk on Christmas Day, at that late-afternoon tipping point when the furnace heat or the too-loud TV or the coughing fits are making you a little crazy. A tinsel bomb, tick-tick-tick. You just have to get out of the house before something explodes.

So when I said, "Hey, anyone for a little hike?" they all rushed to grab their jackets, a sign (I think) of their emerging adult sensibilities.

Now, when I explain this Christmas miracle to other parents, they all say, "Huh, really? Not us."

It can happen, though. After thirty-one years of parenthood, we had the near-perfect holiday season.

The tree didn't fall over—not once. The girls fussed a bit, but not so it mattered. Thing 1 did not even get offended when Thing 2 said something snippy about how she does her eyes.

The boys even helped clean the post-feast kitchen. Not at gunpoint, which is how such chores typically occur. Or by standing around eating the leftover lamb with their fingers while I wash big platters. They actually helped.

It was as if all the parenting books and articles Posh has read over the years coalesced . . . as if a fairy godmother watched over our Christmas, waved her wand (or her Taser), threw pixie dust into the chili, muzzling all cranky childish impulses — theirs and mine.

Yep, a Christmas miracle. Why now? Who knows? Maybe it's an awareness that we can't all stay together forever, that the older kids are bound to branch off in the next few years to stage flawed Christmases of their own.

In any event, we're now one for thirty-one on perfect Christmases. I'm as proud as I am surprised. In its perfection, it stands out from all our other Christmases. As with most perfect things, I don't quite trust it, even as I marvel at its singular beauty.**

"Never again!" I warned them with a wink.

Surely, never again.

### The older daughter responds:
*\* Yet again, this is one of the truer moments that my dad reflects on. In this case, he really did ask my mom if he could clean the house with the leaf blower. The part that he didn't mention was that, to do this, he'd borrow the leaf blower he so thoughtfully and lovingly gave her for Christmas only a few years earlier.*

*\*\* This was definitely a very memorable and sweet Christmas— just the right amount of maturity that finally surfaced out of the younger ones (I've always been mature), and so we got along and were able to do all the things you see families do on TV during the holidays.*

# LAUGH A LITTLE, GIVE MORE

*December 24, 2016*

I've been writing now for forty years, not long. But my goal remains simple: to write something half as good as John Lennon's worst song. Seriously, sometimes I wish he were worse. Sometimes I wish he hadn't set the bar quite so high.

As you may know, I like bars and music and games of chance. I also like Christmas because you never know what you're going to get. Could be an epic season, big and bawdy. Could be a tiny interlude, candlelit and serene.

Yet, in a world brimming with change and disappointment, we can always count on Christmas, a holiday so significant, Tchaikovsky set it to music.*

What's so great about it? Well, how about the simple sound of an acoustic guitar in a crowded church? The clunk of an oven door. Raindrops on roses, whiskers on kittens . . . bright copper kettles . . .

Charles M. Schulz once said of it, "Christmas is doing a little something extra for someone."

So there's that.

I once parked a car for a freaked-out shopper in a crazy Hastings Ranch lot. To be honest, she rammed the curb so many times, I was afraid she might eventually mow us all down. My ultimate goal, every Christmas, is not to wind up as B-roll on CNN.

Years ago, when the kids were quite small, we decided to dress up a little Charlie Brown tree for a beloved elderly neighbor and surprise her with it.

"You want how much for this scrawny thing?" I asked the tree lot attendant.

"Forty."

"Dollars?"

"Forty bucks," he insisted.

"It's a twig," I said. "It's half a %#@*&% pencil."

"Daaaaaaaaaaaaaaaaaaaaaaaaaaaaaaaaaaaaaaaaaaaaaaaaaaaaaaaaad," scolded my lovely and patient older daughter.

All my life, I've been drawn to misfits and malcontents; that's why I had four kids. As I may have mentioned, our hospital has a no-returns policy on babies; they won't even allow exchanges. Doesn't matter—a day, a decade—you can't return them, which is a lousy way to run a hospital, if you ask me.

On that day, in the tree lot, I looked down at my then-ten-year-old daughter—obviously defective, obviously not even my own flesh and blood, for she didn't think that forty bucks was that bad a price for a piece of kindling wood. As every dad knows, $40 is a Christmas ham; $40 is a big bottle of Jack.

"Daaaaaaaaaaaaaaaaaaaaaaaaaaaaaaaaaaaaaaaaaaaaaaaaad," she said.

"Okay, you want it on the roof?" the tree attendant asked as he carried it to the car.

"No, just put it in the glove box," I said.

If you're a father, and the holidays give you the yips and inadvertent twitches, a heightened sense that you're not in control in any way, just laugh at the whole bloody blob of it . . . the excesses, the expectations, the specials that don't seem so special at all.

This year, for instance, Starbucks offered a special fruitcake Frappuccino, perhaps the worst idea since the sitar. Or nuclear weapons. Or even *Bad Santa 2*.

Consider the fruitcake Fraps. They look pre-digested. They look like a cup of moldy socks. Conveniently, little pieces of fruit kept blocking the straw, so you couldn't actually drink it. So laugh.

The holidays are here, so laugh. Plug in a Chevy Chase movie. Call an old pal. Buy your bartender a pair of silly lighted antlers. Laugh.

Because Schulz was right: Christmas is merely doing a little something extra for someone. To that end, the little guy and I are burning homemade cookies together right now. Trust me, someone in the house will eat them.

Look, it's been a long, brutal December here in Los Angeles. Daily highs have rarely broken seventy, and all the women are wearing multiple scarves, as you would a neck brace, and doubling up on designer sweaters to ward off the cruel chill. Forecasters blame a polar vortex. I blame Nordstrom.

Obviously, it is a full-on state of emergency here, and I'm not sure how much more of this the townsfolk can take. Certainly, Santa won't come within 300 miles of a place like this, nor should any of us.**

So, if Santa's a no-show, you might pick up some of the slack. Do that little extra something. Give a humble tree. Or a tray of homemade cookies. How about a bowl of overseasoned meatballs (is there a more succulent holiday sight?).

For in a world chronically short of kindness and charity, at least we'll always have the holidays, at least we'll always have meatballs.

And doorbells and sleigh bells . . . and schnitzel with noodles.

Merry Christmas.

* **The columnist adds:**
*I like that line. I'll probably use it again.*

** **The older daughter says:**
*For all my father's cynicism—much of which I was oh-so-fortunate to inherit—the holidays do have a way of turning him into a big ball of emotion. Sure, he can have a tendency to mourn the lack of snow he reminisces about from the Midwest*

*Christmases of his childhood, lament the summertime-like heat, or wonder why his wife always overfills the entire living room with gifts. But he does spend most of the holiday season thinking about thoughtful gifts to give, the people without families we can invite over on Christmas Eve, and the elderly neighbors whose homes we should help decorate. His mother loved the holidays and always had one of the most festive homes and a tree that glistened from every angle. He really did inherit that holiday spirit, and I'm happy to say that—despite the cynicism—I think I may have, too.*

# EASTER WITH EXPLODING EGGS

*April 22, 2017*

When the kids were really young, we used to have the best Easters. I'd dress up like Jesus, and they'd dress like little Roman soldiers and chase me around the yard. Insert your own symbolism, if you like, but I caution you not to jump to conclusions. Many families have their special traditions.

Mainly, the simple reenactment was just to mark the historical significance of the day and to remind the children about martyrs, intolerance, and rash judgments. I think it worked.

To this day, we like to keep our holidays low-key. No sense making too much fuss. Better to quietly count your blessings — if you happen to have any. No? Just look a little.

If you have children, you have blessings. If you have friends, you have blessings as well.

If you have a nice new Ferrari, that's a blessing I'd like to borrow some Sunday when you're not using it.*

If you have a dog, you have big-time blessings. Dogs are like supergrateful children. In fact, they're better than children, in that they never turn into sullen teenagers. One day soon, dogs will replace children. To walk through downtown LA is to wonder if they might already have.

I swear, there are restaurants in many American cities that require you to have a dog at your table . . . like a dress code.

It's the most wonderful, weirdest, almost spiritual sensation to take a mouthful of omelet just as some strange beast from another table decides at that very moment to lick the jelly from your bare ankle. Honestly, I've had first dates that went far worse.

We had dogs at our Easter table—that's a tradition as well. Brunch was the best. The little guy somehow exploded an undercooked hard-boiled egg in his hand, a comic moment in an otherwise somber celebration bathed in piety.**

"You crack me up," I told him.

"I have egg on my face," he explained.

"We have the weirdest family," the younger daughter said with a sigh.

"I don't know how that happened," said Posh, who, in decades of cooking, has barely bungled a single thing, let alone a hard-boiled egg.

Somehow we recovered from that in time to eat too much again a few hours later, including a kale salad that really wasn't half bad. The older boy grew it in the backyard: farm to fam. Much of what America now eats used to be considered weeds, though I didn't mention that at Easter dinner.

I've learned that I can't say everything that comes into my head, except at work. So many of our holidays are ruined when some little observation is taken the wrong way and someone else overreacts. There's almost a sport to it.

At that point, Posh usually locks herself in the bathroom and refuses to come out.

Knock-knock. Mom? Mom, are you still in there? Dad wants to know if it's okay to serve the pie?

This Easter was not without incident. After dinner, the Russian puppy cornered a helium balloon under a coffee table. She barked and barked, not knowing for sure whether she should kill the darn thing herself or just hold it at bay till police arrived.

I don't speak Russian, but the puppy's basic message seemed to be: "I've cornered this dangerous helium balloon. Someone grab a gun."

Evidently, they don't have helium, or balloons, at the North Pole, where the little Siberian husky was born. She barked at it for almost an hour, till someone threw a dinner fork at the balloon. That's how we Irish solve most problems. We hurl things. Works about as well as anything.

Knock-knock. Mom? Mom, it's me again. Just so you know, the puppy got hold of the ham . . . .

So, yeah, we're making a big point lately of counting our blessings, amid some current domestic challenges. Termites attacked the back porch last week, gobbled it like soft hot cheese. And the old clothes dryer finally gave out with a billion socks on the odometer.

Posh looked and looked to find a replacement that would fit in the custom cabinet. She finally found a very stylish little dryer—I think it's European—that may do the trick. It also doubles as a bread maker. Leave it to the French, huh?

Cost us $1,000 for the dryer/bread maker and $400 more just to run a new circuit. Then some component in the overpriced oven went out; that was 600 bucks.

Adversity is inevitable—like heartbreak, like bungled Easter eggs, like feasting termites. All inevitable. But we have much to be thankful for this spring, let's just leave it at that.

Knock-knock-knock. Mom?

* **The little guy responds:**
*Me too!*

** **He adds:**
*I remember that! You made it seem not that funny.*

**The columnist explains:**
*Son, that's what I do.*

# ON THE ROAD

# BACK IN THE HEARTLAND

*August 26, 2004*

We traveled to Chicago in the roughest of ways. We flew commercial.

At LAX, there was a man wearing capri pants, ankle-length slacks of the kind Bobbie Jo wore on these old episodes of *Petticoat Junction*. It's just the sort of sight that keeps me from traveling much. In another year or two, I probably won't even leave my bedroom.

"Want some latte?" the older daughter offers while we await our flight.

"It's not very hot," I say after a sip.

"It's exactly 150 degrees," she says. "I ordered it special."

It's good that we live in a nation where you can do that. We can't control our borders. We can't teach our children algebra. But we can order coffee drinks at the temperature of our choice. I guess you have to start somewhere.

"Can I go get a Cinnabon?" the little girl asks.

"Where?"

"Terminal 2," she says.

In this day and age, some people are intimidated by flying. Not the ones I live with.

While we await our flight, they visit every corner of this vast airport. They chat up the salespeople, sample the drinking fountains, salute every passing pilot.

Traveling with them is like accompanying a band of Amish children, excited by every simple thing. Aboard the plane, after the instructional video ends, they all applaud it.

"Oh, my God," I tell my wife when the clapping dies down.

"It's only a five-hour flight," she says, which might be the least soothing thing anyone has ever said to me.

First, a few apologies. To the passenger in seat 20D, directly in front of us, who midway through the flight enjoyed the lovely sensation of a one-year-old's sticky fingers combing his thinning hair.

Or to the pilot, who high over South Dakota announced that we were experiencing some "clear air turbulence." It was really just one of my kids closing the tray table much too hard, over and over and over.

And most of all, to me, in seat 21F, who had to change the baby's toxic diaper—I know not how—in the space between me and the seat in front of us. Like Houdini, I don't fully understand how I'm able to pull off many of my better tricks.

In the end, of course, this Con Air flight was well worth it. For we finally landed in this endearing little metropolis by the lake, where their grandmother and cousins live, a forty-cent toll ride from O'Hare.

Here on the outskirts of Chicago, there are farms and hay trucks and big mansions where other farms once stood. Fish jump with joy in the lakes, and the people have these creamy complexions that come from steady diets of good cheese, cold beer, and the occasional cigarette. And those are just the grandmas.

"Can we move here?" the little girl asks.

I stand in the backyard of the house my father built, turning brats on the grill and watching the way the sun glints off the antenna on the rooftop next door, just as it did back in 1971.

"See, it looks like an airplane," says my mother.

"Yep," I say.

"It's like that every August," she says.

As the bratwurst hisses, I listen to the train horns I was raised on and the church bells that signal happy hour each day at five. I hear the high school marching band, rehearsing Big Ten fight songs a mile away, the best fight songs of all.

Can we move here? Why the heck not.

"That nice place across the street?" someone says during a cocktail party the next night.

"Yes?"

"Sold for almost $300,000," she says.

"That's insane," someone else says.

It is insane. From a California perspective, insanely cheap. The urge is to cash out back in LA and live mortgage-free here in the mighty Middle West. In time, we could probably snag tickets to Cubs games, which seem always sold out. Wrigley is becoming the Parthenon of sports complexes, more revered with each fallen brick.

And if we moved back, we'd have four seasons again. I was raised on weather and always miss it. Life's more interesting when Tuesday is different from Wednesday. November different from March.

But I fear this town where I grew up may have changed far too much. Where barbershops once stood, now there are stockbroker offices. Instead of hardware stores, there are children's boutiques no one can afford.

And each evening at six, well-dressed professionals squeeze out of the commuter trains with that awful, soulless gaze you see on riders getting off any sort of overcrowded mass transit. The worst part: I don't recognize a single face.

Do our hometowns ever get better over time? Probably not. Hopefully, that'll never keep us from coming back to visit.

"Look at that sky," the boy says, pointing at buttermilk clouds.

"I love it here," the older daughter says.

Me, too.

# YOUR TOILET HAS MORE TROUT

*August 21, 2003*

There's this one quiet afternoon in the hammock I won't forget, just one, in our vacation week in the woods. A book. A drink. A gentle breeze nuzzling the aspen. Next thing I know, they're placing a baby in my lap.

"Who's this?" I ask.

"Your son."

Likely story.

People are always trying to palm their children off on me. I gladly accept, but not naively. I know what kids can do to your life. I know how they'll hijack your soul.

"Here, kid, listen to this," I tell the baby as I open the book I've been waiting three days to read.

"Snipe came up behind her and wrapped his arms around her waist, pressed his sallow face against her hot back. She smelled of road dust, of golden rod, and crushed blackberries; her humming voice vibrated in his ear."

At hearing this, the baby twists next to me like a cat, head in my armpit. He finds it's the best way to enjoy modern literature. I turn a page. He twists some more.

"Lucky Snipe," the baby's probably thinking. "Read some more, Dad."

"Haylett was down the next morning at 3:30 to get the stove going. He liked turning the dark chill away, enjoyed the little solitude, the resinous odor of kindling catching fire. The shovel squeaked as he drew out the ashes."

The baby and I decided several months ago that we'd skip the traditional infant books and dive headfirst into serious adult fiction. Neither of us has ever looked back. On this day, we spend an hour swinging in the hammock and listening to each other's stomach noises.

"Catch any fish?" they always ask when we return from vacation. But they never ask about hammock time.

Of course, we did spend countless hours on the banks of a beautiful river, trying to stitch on fishhooks in the twilight, onto line as slender as a baby's eyelash.

"Ready, Dad?"

"No."

"How about now?"

"No."

With fishing gear, I have a surgeon's steady hand but the sorry eyes of a cartoon cop. In the fading light, I can barely make out the hook, let alone the hint of fishing line. Got it? Nope. Got it? Nope. I may as well be placing angels on the head of a pin.

That's not the worst of it. When the hook finally hits the water, the brittle fishing line explodes like an Alka-Seltzer, into a snarl within a snarl, into Harpo Marx's hair.

"Catch any fish?" your friends always ask when you return, as if that were ever an option.

No, for the record we caught no fish, though we did spend $120 on various California fishing licenses—far more than the average Sacramento bribe—and went out fishing four times, to granite-bottomed lakes and rivers. Believe me, your bathtub has more marine life. Your toilet has more trout.

No, we recorded nary a bite, unless you count the mosquito welts running halfway up my leg. Honeymoon hickeys aren't this big. Every midnight, I crave a skin graft and a shot of whiskey.

"I think it's a Hemingway thing," their mother explains as we trudge home from fishing, glum and swollen and scented by bait.

"Who?" asks one of the kids.

"Hemingway," repeats their mom.

"Mariel?" asks the older daughter.

Nope, there were no fish this vacation, but no regrets either, except maybe for the overspending, overdrinking, and oversleeping, all of which were tied together one way or another, a chain reaction of summer's over-indulgences.*

"Ever mail those postcards?" I ask my wife as we finally head out of town after our week in the mountains.

"No."

"We'll mail them next year," I say.

So we roll back down the mountain, my wife and her bargain-basement Hemingway, heading home to a world with eight area codes and fourteen freeways. Returning to back-to-school sales and soccer meetings, dead lawns and neighbors we've never met. Worst of all, no quiet time.

"You never see hammocks in LA," I told Posh one day in the mountains. "I've never seen one hammock."

"What's a hammock?" she says.

"See?"

Up the Grapevine, down the Grapevine, the car coughing on the smog on our re-entry to Earth, the kids eating cold French fries and dreading school. Smelling of road dust and blackberries.

Home, we've come, but not eagerly. Home . . . with vacation pictures that will outlast the Visa bills and memories clearer than Kodachrome.

"Catch any fish?" they'll all want to know.

Yeah, a million.

\* The older daughter remembers:

*Our family took this summer trip to Lake Tahoe a few years in a row, and it became a family favorite. This doesn't do justice to the bonding time and relaxation it offered, but it does sum up some moments perfectly. My dad has been hoping to re-create one of these trips again soon with all of us as adults.*

# THAT'S LONDON CALLING

*May 9, 2009*

A wonderful thing, a daughter. It's what the creator gave me instead of a way with money or a firm jawline. I have two daughters, the oldest of whom is accompanying me to London for a week of work. She is lovely. She is patient. She is . . . gasp . . . twenty-five?

"I-can't-wait, I-can't-wait, I-can't-wait," she says a few days before we leave.

She talks that way, briskly, so that the words run together to form contractions. I understand only half of what she says. I become jet-lagged and dizzy just from hearing her speak.

But we get along well, she and I. There is a sort of mutual respect. She is the oldest of the siblings; I am the oldest of the parents. We both understand the rigors of seniority.

Before we depart, I lay out the ground rules for the big trip:

☞ I occasionally need and enjoy a nice nap.

☞ I don't drink during the brightness of day or the pitch black of night. I drink in that dreamy netherworld between sunlight and darkness, usually starting at 4 p.m. and running till about 8. I do so with dignity and honor.

☞ In a new city, I talk to everyone—cops, bartenders, muggers, millionaires. Some people are put off by this. I don't care. I once had a two-hour chat with an old guy in a stamp shop ("Hey, where'd you get that great sweater?").

☞ I never ever buy souvenirs, but I have a weakness for any sort of street food and will always leave a buck or two to street musicians, even drop a fiver in the hat if they are any good. It's my way of supporting the arts.

☞ I like to eat where the locals eat and—to soak up color—rely almost exclusively on public transit.

☞ I travel light, with two pairs of jeans, one pair of dress slacks, five T-shirts, and a sport coat I've had since 1987, a tweed jobber that you can wad up into a pillow on an airplane or a jail cot and it will spring back to life unaffected. I think it is thirty percent rubber. It is the best sport coat a man ever owned.

☞ I get up early and go to bed in the wee hours—sometimes as late as ten o'clock.

☞ I'm told I snore a little.

That's it. Besides those little quirks—I call them my principles of hearty travel—I have zero demands on my travel mate, other than to have a good time, for vacation is therapy, a brandy for the brain.

The lovely and patient older daughter seems okay with these guidelines, even though her siblings scoff at them and fear openly about her journey with Dad.

Being young, they have never encountered a man with principles before.

"I-can't-wait, I-can't-wait, I-can't-wait," she says again, like a mantra.

"Are you sure?"

"I-can't-wait," she says.

Okay, so we go, out of my favorite airport, LA-HEX. After nearly a dozen hours in steerage (limited toilet use, poor food), we land in London-town, renowned for its sordid and hasty royal weddings (a topic I know a little something about).

And we are off . . .

We take London like two Vikings. I like to lead the way, but so does the lovely and patient older daughter. As the eldest of four, she doesn't like to wait for other people to make decisions. By sheer will, she can change stoplights and get waiters to bring us more bread.

On the frenetic London streets, my daughter dashes this way and that. She is proud of how assertive she has become, a trait she links to growing up in Los Angeles, a trait I link to the boiling bloodlines of her dear mum.

"This way, Dad," she says.

"No, this way," I say.

In a crowd of ten thousand screaming idiots at Buckingham Palace, I find her, then lose her, then find her again.

Fortunately, the sun hits her like an autumn day. I can locate her in a crowd just by the chestnut in her hair, the reds and browns of mid-October.

"If I lose you, we'll meet back at the hotel," I tell her at one point, fearing we'll get swept apart in a crowd, then spend too long looking for each other when we should be enjoying the sights.

"How about we meet at the subway platform?" she says.

"Back at the hotel," I say.

"The platform."

"The hotel."

It is our only real argument, though I do scold her for pulling out her iPhone during a profoundly stirring service at Westminster, then the next evening in a spectacularly ancient English theater.

"You need cellphone rehab," I tell her later.

"I know," she says sheepishly.

At times, I want to throw the damn iPhone into the Thames, so hooked is she on its little screen and messages from her buddies back in the States.

But I don't.

A daughter is a gift, remember? No refunds, no returns.

**The lovely and patient older daughter responds:**
*While it took twenty-five years of my life before I was able to mooch a trip without any of the others tagging along, it was oh-so-worth it. Every stranger my dad talked to, every beer he sipped, every bite of street food he savored, and every nap he insisted on (often in the grass outside of an art gallery I'd drag him through) all made me realize just how similar we are. Sure, we have our diffeences. While I talk fast, he talks loud. While he doesn't pack underwear, I pack countless shoes. While I rely on my phone's map to get us to the right place (that's why I used it so much—I swear!), he wanders a little more. But I encourage every parent and child to escape on a trip alone like we were lucky enough to do. It's a fantastic bonding moment, and my dad— through often-thick sarcasm and quick wit—depicted this moment in our lives with more truth and less embellishment than usual, which makes it an extra-special story for me to revisit.*

## SPRING TRAINING WITH HOWARD

*March 13, 2013*

PHOENIX—Let me tell you about Josh Hamilton's first rocket ship of spring. It isn't a perfect home run. He gets under it a bit more than he would've liked, so it's towering, corpulent, full of cha-cha.

At last sighting, it was in geosynchronous orbit with Earth. NBC was about to bounce Brian Williams's evening newscasts off of it, and someone at Palomar was pronouncing it a planet.

So no, it wasn't a perfect home run by any means. But it got your attention, all right. It was the kind of celestial event befitting the newest Angel.

In our last installment, we were screaming across the desert on the way to spring training, my buddy Howard with his head out the window panting in anticipation, which is not the most efficient way to fly, but sometimes you just suck it up.

Howard's old, but he's big and somewhat menacing. I think he stole the Gideon Bible from the Motel 6, and the coffee maker went missing, too. Or maybe there wasn't a coffee maker. But there definitely was a Gideon Bible. It was the kind of place that needed one—cigarette burns on the bathtub, the bedspreads smelling of mule.

I can't seem to find decent lodging in Tempe, no matter what. Next time, I'm sleeping in center field.

Anyway, I'm sure there'll be a next time because these road trips will be a rite of spring from here on out. There is no better way to drink too much, stay up too late, and otherwise become emotionally unstable in anticipation of the approaching baseball season. Fans need to train, too, you know.*

One night, we find ourselves in Don & Charlie's, my favorite Phoenix watering hole/rib joint. Don & Charlie's makes a martini the size of a fish tank. Mine came with a carp.

Also on this menu: Ned Colletti Chicken Schnitzel. I didn't even know you could schnitzel a chicken, but I guess it depends on how much the chicken has had to drink.

We've moved east since our overnight at Camelback, camping in Tempe in anticipation of an Angels spring game. Half the Angels roster this year could end up in either the Hall of Fame or rehab, depending on which way they want to play things. For now, we'll remain optimistic.

Rocket blasts like Hamilton's make it easy to do that. And speaking of corpulent things, Mike Trout isn't nearly as bloated as you might hope, were you a humorist looking to poke fun at prematurely blubbery ball-players. Actually, he carries the weight very well.

In fact, we should all carry excess weight like Trout. He has the gliding trot of a Heisman-winning back. Some of the old-timers, going as far back as 1985, say he reminds them of Bo Jackson. Zeus is also mentioned.

What a pitcher's nightmare this Angels lineup is, with Trout teeing off first, soon followed by Pujols, Hamilton. Also pencil in Howie Kendrick somewhere, for he seems to be swatting everything that moves.

The classiest guy on staff is Hank Conger, who stops patiently for autographs on the way out of a morning workout.

Angels tip No. 1: Best autograph opportunity is at the edge of the parking lot just after morning workouts, usually around 11:45, or if manager Mike Scioscia is a little grumpy, almost 2 p.m.

Tip No. 2: Best tanning spot at Diablo Stadium is the picnic tables along the left-field line, where a fine grilled tri-tip sandwich runs $8.

Tip No. 3: Best shady spot is row P and up, from behind the backstop and along the first-base line.

Wow, that's a lot of information for one little column. The irony is that, like Trout, they pay me mostly in hot dogs.

We're back on the road heading home, after two long days in the Arizona sun, a state that doesn't need a governor; it needs a state dermatologist.

Fortunately, I'm still the kind of kid who buys cars based on the sound system. Mid-desert, we're out of radio range, the CDs are blaring, and Howard (who might have sun stroke) is quoting Leonard Cohen lyrics and talking about how he once sang *Belshazzar's Feast* in church.

"Goes something like this . . ." he says.

We're in a dead zone, all right, somewhere between the liquid optimism of training camp and the hard reality of home.

Okay, Howard, time to get your head in the car.**

<br>

* **Howard responds:**
*Glendale one day (Dodgers vs. Angels), Tempe the next (Angels vs. Dodgers). The preferred common ingredient? Something that Chris labeled "liquid optimism."*

**The columnist responds:**
*Learned about "liquid optimism" as a Cubs fan. Had to.*

** **Howard responds:**
*After three days of marinating in the heat and the juice, my head felt as though Mike Scioscia had used it for a fungo bat. Hence, it simply would not fit back into Erskine's rental car.*

# NATURE OR NURTURE?

*June 28, 2014*

I'm a sucker for summer, when our best memories are made.

On the first day of the season, we drove off west for some sort of baseball solstice in one of those impossibly perfect American suburbs where the kids have too much hair (as if loomed) and all the moms have been enhanced.

Baseball is one percent action and ninety-nine percent idle thought, and it occurs to me during one of those interminable two-hour gaps between batters that kids play baseball today for all the right reasons—not for fun or friendship, but as if someone's life hangs in the balance, as if there's some sort of ransom to be paid.

Of course, I support this. My own kid, forty-seven pounds of grit, freckles, and Band-Aid residue, was born to play pro ball. We gave him his first bat when he was still in the womb—my idea. Took some convincing on my part, but once I got my stubborn wife to sign off, the toughest part was choosing the right bat. Alloy or composite? Big barrel or standard?*

I let her pick the color.

Anyway, that paid off because now our son is batting eleventh in an eleven-man lineup, and we're rising at 5 a.m. on summer's first Saturday in support of his big league career, which seems as inevitable as rain on a Portland parade.

Nature or nurture? Well, we believe in both. The little guy was born to greatness, and we'll insist that he reach for the stars. Either that, or the whole thing with the womb bat will prove to have been just a stupid waste of time.

As always, it was a full day on the ball field. We got battered by our first opponent, then smothered by the second, yet there were teachable moments throughout, such as discovering that the tri-tip sandwich at the snack bar was the size of a Mazda.

The same way Bach layered in violins, that's how they layered in the beef, charred strips of perfectly roasted California sirloin. In such a way, the sting of life's little disappointments can quickly be forgotten.

Ah, baseball, the ultimate metaphor—bad hops, lousy luck, and the occasional miracle. Could anything be worse?

First there's the game itself—the foul tips off your ankle, the ground balls crazy off your knee. Then there's the parents, the passive-aggressive agents of any youth league. And don't forget our boys of summer, who have received relentless poundings from bigger boys from bigger cities. After two months of this, they are dusty, they are sad.**

Me, I think all parents see their child as a little better than he or she actually is. Parenthood is a tricky prism, and we're all a little nearsighted about our own kids. Children shouldn't be human trophies.

In any case, athletic greatness was probably decided by God or science at the moment of conception. But go ahead, push your kid. See how that works out for you. In twenty-five years of this, I've seen only one of my kids' teammates go on to a pro career, and he washed out after a couple of years—after his arm fell clear off his body.

"Summer has filled her veins with light and her heart is washed with noon," wrote British poet Cecil Day-Lewis.

And youth sports can scorch our parental souls.

Sunday was more of the same, baseball balmed by tri-tip, then a beery World Cup soccer match, followed by a sundown concert in a park near home.

As is usually the case, the free concert in the park begins with the wives and husbands integrated around a table. Then the moms go off to one end and the dads to the other, presumably to talk more freely, or at least in a similar dialect.

The more I deal with women, the less I understand them. Besides, the guys are less likely to talk about just the kids, the way the women do, though inevitably everything has to come back around to the children, this being a suburb's most important cash crop.

"After he pulled his tooth, I went in the bathroom and it was like the Crimea," my buddy Andy says of his son's attempt at self-dentistry.

So there's a summer weekend—baseball, picnics, bloodshed. It's the rituals I love, not the outcomes. After all, how many summers do you get? Seventy? A hundred? Where once there seemed so many, there now seem so few.

They're sweeter when they're properly played.

**The little guy responds:**
* *That's funny, Dad. But too much detail?*
** *Yeah, baseball hurts. It's fun and frustrating—equal parts.*

# FATHERS & DAUGHTERS

# ELBOWS UP, BUTTS DOWN

*March 3, 2005*

Here we are again in shallow right field, planting the seeds of hope, accomplishment, and satire for an entire softball season to come, fixing bad swings and correcting unsteady smiles. The suburbs, they can be a lot of work, you know.

"Elbows up, girls," I say over and over again. "Elbows waaaaaay up."

Change comes hard to the aggressive children of successful parents. Willful. Confident. Frighteningly verbal. Eager listeners, too—if only to one another. Why change anything when life has been so good already? Right away, I sense we have our work cut out for us.

"Butt down," I say. "On grounders, you've got to get your fannies down."

We are in the early stages of a relationship, the team and I, and the girls still aren't sure whether I really know anything more than a few simple commands. "Who is this guy?" they wonder among themselves. "Is it really legal to say *butt* in public?"

So they turn their freckles to the sun. Smile a little. Get their butts down and their elbows up. You know, just in case we're right about something.

"Peyton, get that elbow up," I say again.

"Okay, coach," she says.

I'm a coach of unusual specifications. Athletically gifted. Mentally large. Like most men, I'm prone to machine-gun bursts of advice, then long, mournful periods of silence. What more could you ask of a coach? Even Lombardi shut up once in a while.

"Kate?" I say.

"What, coach?"

"How many hands do you have?"

"Two."

"Well, use 'em both," I say.

"Okay, coach," she says, smiling.

We refuse to coddle them, these twelve- and thirteen-year-old daughters of suburban America. They come to us pre-coddled, many of them. We'll teach them, praise them, and tease them into shape. But we won't coddle. Too much coddling can ruin a kid.*

And so far, such toughness is proving valuable. At the very first batting practice, I caught a whiffle ball in my tender, underutilized reproductive region. In a way, it was a relief, since each season I sustain some career-threatening injury, and it's always good to take your lumps early.

Last year, for example, I bumped an elbow on a dugout post and had to drink left-handed for a week. Do you have any idea how much weight you can lose when you have to eat and drink with your opposite hand? Well, not enough. But some.

"What do you want me to work on now?" asks Steve, my dedicated coaching colleague.

"My taxes?"

"How about stealing?" he says.

"Same thing," I say.

The girls love to practice stealing. Second base. Home. They don't care.

How deliciously subversive stealing is. How honest and up-front. When you steal a base, you go in feet first and with a clear conscience. How many fun things can you say that about anymore?

"Good slide, Anna," I say.

"Thanks, coach."

"Next!" I yell.

"Me?" Jessica asks.

"Why not," I say.

The annual player draft went well, with nary a complaint. It just goes to show what well-meaning people can accomplish when they set aside their personal agendas for the good of the group. For a week after, there were a few scattered shootings. A house was torched. Nothing out of the ordinary. **

"Why do I keep doing this?" I ask my buddy Paul.

"Because you're a junkie," he says.

"I don't get it," I say.

"You're mainlining misery," he explains.

Such is the price of strong leadership. Churchill wasn't always beloved. And they eventually shot Lincoln, of course. Little League is politics without decorum. The stakes, evidently, far higher.

But the results, so far, have been splendid. All the teams in our league appear to have chemistry, charisma, and the sort of brash, ponytailed swagger you love to see in young ball clubs. They scurry around the bases as if they eat nothing but semisweet baker's chocolate. Hair in their eyes? Doesn't matter.

"Dad, what time is it?" the little girl asks.

"2:05," I say.

"2:05 or 2:07?" she asks.

"Why?"

"Because sometimes you round down," she says.

"2:15," I say.

Yep, sometimes we round down, just to get in a few more minutes of infield practice. In this town, actresses shave years off their ages and coaches round down. Nobody really seems to mind. We're just trying to squeeze a few more minutes out of our short careers.

Because Sofia looks to have a very promising swing, serious as Oedipus. Erin can make the throw all the way from third, triggering memories of

Santo. Lynn? Quick as a bumblebee.

"You look good, coach," one of the fathers says.

"You exaggerate," I say.

"No," he says. "You look good."

Such is spring, a season of exaggeration and fresh starts. When everyone is undefeated and the damp grass smells like lunch.

Spring. Renewal. Hope. Desperation.

Butts down, girls. Elbows up.

* **The daughter responds:**
*Really, he was an easy coach. Except when he yelled at me to "STOP STANDING THERE LIKE A STATUE!" during a soccer game. I haven't forgiven him.*

**The columnist responds:**
*I've forgiven you, though. But it was like you were set in concrete.*

** **The daughter adds:**
*Oh, to be a fly on the wall at that draft.*

# OH, HEAVENLY FATHER . . .

*December 16, 2004*

Here we are in youth soccer playoffs, in the second shoot-out in two weeks. If you don't know what a shoot-out is, let me just say that it's no place for children. It is a goofy, capricious method for determining an outcome after a tie game. To oversimplify, each team takes five penalty shots; the team that makes the most shots wins. It would be like determining a bitter divorce with pistols at twenty paces. Okay, bad example. Some folks would actually enjoy that.

"Come on, let's pray," Taylor says before the tiebreaker begins.

"Yeah, let's pray," says Lindsay.

I don't know what AYSO's policy is on prayer circles before shoot-outs. Certainly, they have a rule somewhere. They have rules everywhere. The prayer circle is probably determined by some sort of coin flip. The leader probably has to stand on the north side of the field, facing God.

"Oh heavenly father . . . " Taylor begins.

I loiter a few yards from the prayer circle because I don't really want the parents, twenty yards away, to get wind that I am allowing the girls to join hands and say a prayer.

I have no problem with what they are doing, of course, but what kind of world would we have if children from all different backgrounds and religions just suddenly joined hands and started praying together for strength, peace, and good fortune? Some people might be furious.

"Please help us be brave and do our best," Taylor says.

"And guide the ball into the net," says Emily.

"Yeah, especially that," Becca says.

"Amen," says Lindsay.

When we last checked in on the mighty Glow Chicks, they were just beginning a long season of soccer with the highest of hopes. Their uniforms were bright, almost glowing. Their hair never looked better.

Oh sure, skin care issues arose from time to time, and certainly fashion was important, but for the twelve- and thirteen-year-old Glow Chicks, their hair trumped all other concerns. The way it looked, the way it fell across their eyes, obscuring anything they might do on a soccer field.

"My bangs, like, just exploded," one girl said at practice one night.

"Exploded?"

"Bang!" said someone else.

Which resulted in waves of convulsive, belly-aching laughter. Because in addition to the importance of hair, and the importance of prayer, the Glow Chicks were firm believers—all of them—of the therapeutic effects of laughing astoundingly hard on a regular basis.

"This one time, in science class . . ." Kelsey would begin.

"Oh my God, I remember that!" Lucy would shout, and grunting, glorious fits of laughter would follow.

Sometimes, hair and laughter would come together. On windy days, it was all they could do to keep from suffocating on their own shiny locks, which would blow into their faces when they laughed and ran, no matter how many times they'd swipe at it.

"Forget about your hair, Katie!" I'd yell from the sidelines during games.

"What?"

"Your hair, forget it!"

"Okay, coach!" she'd lie.

Yet, with all these distractions, the Glow Chicks* managed to put together a great season and memories that will last months, at least. We won more than we lost. We laughed more than we cried.

A typical game went something like this.

First quarter: We quickly discover that the referee, a good man and devoted volunteer, may be legally blind. Ray Charles blind. Because he is a good man and devoted volunteer, we are reluctant to complain.

Second quarter: We give up a goal that I fail to see because I'm studying the next quarter's substitutions. "Did you see that foul?" someone asks. Um, no. And neither did the ref—a good man, a devoted volunteer.

Third quarter: The game drags on like a Lutheran wedding. I look down at my clipboard and begin to work on my taxes.

Fourth quarter: We finally score, when Kelsey passes to Aimie, who passes to Holly, who passes to Sarah, who is on the other team actually but mis-kicks it to Carolyn, whose shot starts to go wide but is pulled back into line by one of Earth's natural magnetic fields.

"That's just good coaching," I'd point out after any sort of freak goal.

"You should get a big raise," some wise guy would say, usually Larry.

Actually. I should get two raises. Because now it's come down to this: a tense shoot-out at the end of regulation. Five girls. Five kicks. If we win, we play next week. We lose, we're done for the season.

"Just do your best," I tell them.

"Yeah, and don't screw up," says Anna.

"Come on, let's pray," Taylor says, and then the prayer circle begins.

As for the final result, let's just leave it at this: Some things in life don't work out. Sometimes, strong kicks go high over the crossbar, good shots sail wide, even prayers fall short.**

But the loud, wild, and wonderful Glow Chicks will always remind us of one little thing. A good, gasping laugh is still the best form of exercise, one of God's great gifts.

Better even, than soccer itself.

**\* The daughter responds:**
*Why was it okay for this to be our team name?*

**The columnist responds:**
*You and your teammates chose the name. We once had a team called the Runny Eggs because our uniforms were yolk yellow and we liked to run. Generally, AYSO names make no sense. It's an American tradition.*

**\*\* The daughter adds:**
*What Dad left out was that I missed the penalty kick and we lost the game.*

**The columnist responds:**
*I am so over that. It took years, but I am totally over that.*

## LOVELY? PATIENT? PUH-LEEZE!

*June 21, 2007*

My dad took Father's Day off and asked me to write his column for him again. Father's Day. What a thing to celebrate.

"You're the Dorothy Parker of the suburbs," he says.

"Who's she, Dad?"

"Never mind," he snorts, and goes back to watching the Weather Channel.

You probably don't remember me. I'm the older daughter, the lovely and patient one. I don't know if my dad is being all ironic or what when he calls me that. Seriously, without me, this house would fall apart. I'm the mortar between the bricks. I'm the icing on a seven-layer crazy cake.*

Right now, my dad is on the couch with my two brothers. They are watching TV and making clucky noises with their tongues. They sound like three monkeys with peanut butter stuck to the roofs of their mouths.

"Dad!" I scream.

"Yes?"

"Quit clucking!"

"We're just practicing our jungle noises," my dad explains.

"Cluck-cluck-cluck-cluck-cluck," clucks my little brother.

It's been even weirder than usual around here lately. Dad says he thinks "the marriage is played out" and that twenty-five years is all that anyone should have to suffer, "particularly a nice woman like your mother."

Mom says marriage is "an antiquated institution that betrays our Calvinist heritage."

"But it sure beats the crap out of dating again," says my dad.

"That's for sure," says Mom.

Isn't love, you know, kind of amazing?

All I can say is it's good they have their own separate interests. In my mom's case, it's herself. In my dad's case, it's working on the house. He says our house used to be one of those little drive-through huts where you could buy gum and smokes. So I guess it needs a little work.

Every weekend he's out in the backyard fixing things up. When a project goes badly, he flings stuff. When it goes well, he whistles old Tijuana Brass songs. Pretty much all the songs he likes date from the early 1700s.

Seriously, this is what my dad thinks: He thinks Herb Alpert was partly responsible for the sexual revolution, "on account of the sensuality and lyricism of his many songs."

"In a sense, you're Herb Alpert's daughter," he says.

"Um, yuck," I say.

My dad says that he was probably born fifty years too late and would've preferred an era where everybody mowed their own lawn and TV had just three channels, all in black and white.

"What's black and white?" my sister asks him

"Those are the two primary colors," says my brother.

"No, they're not," my sister shrieks.

"Well, they're important, that's all I know," says my brother.

Once upon a time, Dad says, all of America's entertainment options were in black and white. Then color TVs started coming out and ruined everything.

"Although *Laugh-In* was pretty good," says my dad.

"I also liked *Love, American Style*," says my mom.

Oh my God, we are like a distant wing of the Smithsonian Institution, except there are no buses or group tours.

When I point this out, Dad says we are all very fortunate to live in a house with a sense of history, even if it's a little twisted. Mom says he's just trying to be provocative and get a rise out of me.

"Don't let him get to you," she says.

"Mom, he's crazy!" I say.

"Yes, but he helped you move, didn't he?" she reminds me.

Yeah, he's good with that. I've moved, like, nine times in the last six years, on account of college and stuff. Meanwhile, I spend a lot of nights here at home, since my little brother is only four and does cute stuff all the time.

"He is soooooo adorable," all my friends say.

"He got that from me," says my dad.

Oh my God, did I tell you about this? You know that new lawn my dad is putting in out back? Well anyway, every morning he wakes up to find that raccoons have flipped over the sod to look for grubs and stuff. I guess what happens is that they get the munchies in the middle of the night, and wormy things taste good to them. Sort of like raccoon sushi. Yum.

"Varmints!" Dad says when he looks out each morning to see the sod all messed up.

"It's us against them," says my mom.

"You mean the kids?"

"No, the raccoons," she says, and they stand at the back window staring out, wondering what they'll do next.

I think that pretty much sums up parenthood, standing with an arm around each other and trying to figure out what to do next. I mean, I guess that's a life—twenty-five years of kids, bills, car repairs, and curfews. Twenty-five years of varmints, with no end in sight. Tick-tock, tick-tock, tick-tock. . . .

Me, I'm betting on the varmints.

**\* The columnist adds:**

*Readers often ask whether my older daughter actually wrote the columns where she allegedly subs for me. All I can say is I don't remember writing them myself.*

**The daughter responds:**

*I've been asked countless times if I actually write these columns. For those still wondering: The answer is no. This is the first time I'm getting to have a voice in any of this. Two years into my own career, I did finally have to tell my dad he couldn't keep pretending to be me so this may likely be the last of its kind or one of the last. Either way, he does manage to get enough of my perspective in—although the language is not my own words. My dad, that summer, did resemble Bill Murray in* Caddyshack.

**The columnist adds:**

*She's always been the funny one.*

# ANOTHER FENDER BENDER

*February 7, 2015*

Let's catch up with one of the children, some of whom aren't quite children anymore, though we will always worry for them a tad too much.

One of them got rear-ended the other day while stopped at the freeway exit ramp. When she called, my first question was, "Are you all right?"*

Looking back, I was proud of the reaction, for given my usual abruptness and inherent fear of insurance adjusters, I could easily have blurted out: "How bad is it?!"

Instead, I inquired as to her health and general well-being. Was her neck okay? Could she touch her toes? Yes, she said.

And I was proud of the way my twenty-three-year-old handled the incident. It was only her fourth minor accident, yet she knew to get insurance info and a selfie with the other driver's license.

Through it all, my daughter was a little rattled but not upset. She didn't cry. Tears come easily to her. On the right occasion, she wears them like jewelry.

Note that it was me she called, not her mother, which is a bit of an aberration. Her mother is her go-to parent in times of need—her emotional duct tape.

In short, an easy mark.

Their relationship is almost sisterly: They cocoon on the couch eating gelato together under the winter blankets and can spend an entire Saturday afternoon returning a single pair of shoes.

Generally, it goes like this: First, she and Posh have lunch, then they stop for coffee, after which they'll explore "that cute little shop that sells artisanal pasta." If the day hasn't gotten away from them, they'll maybe make it to the mall to return the shoes.**

Otherwise, they put off returning the shoes until the following weekend, when the entire cycle begins again. One time, returning a pair of shoes lasted an entire year and cost an estimated $25,000 in artisanal pastas. I bolt awake at night at the thought of these two planning a wedding.

So, as you can see, it was an honor that she called. On the phone, my daughter was mostly polite, addressing me as "Mr. Erskine" several times.

"How bad is it?" I finally blurted.

"It's okay, Mr. Erskine," my daughter said. "The car's okay."

I'm still having trouble sleeping, and the usual solutions—thoughts of draining three-pointers against the Celtics or chasing a young Angie Dickinson through Paris on a moped—haven't helped as much as you might imagine.

Before the accident, I'd already had a full plate. For months, I've been fretting for a sick friend, and just when he was back eating cheeseburgers and being a general pain in the *tookus* once again, our adjustable mortgage jumped 0.75 percentage point—a quiver, a caress. Yet it goosed the monthly payment by $700.

As it was, we were barely cutting it. I fear we will be priced out of California soon. Good riddance. It is a splendid place but somewhat overpriced. Besides, who wants to be permanently anchored to a place with so little Greek food?

Next up for us, another country. Greece, for example. I wonder how the schools are? Do they play a lot of Little League? Do they have gyros for breakfast?

Fortunately, the car damage was minimal. It was more of a laugh line than a dent, barely creasing the car's vinyl veneer. The way a long wisp of hair dangles across a pretty cheekbone, that's the way this wrinkle lay across the bumper's plastic shell.

At the very most, it can't cost more than four or five grand to fix. Of course, the Easter bunny will be making me omelets in bed before an insurance company ever calls back. Most likely, I'll have to hound them or hound my daughter about hounding them. In either case, a lot of hounding will occur.

In the end, I'll end up lunging into the phone, screaming, "Are you kidding me?" to everything they say.

Still, I see this little fender bender as a blessing, not a curse, and a good test for my continued emotional development.

I've been very leery lately of what I call "panicked parenting," by which moms and dads treat child-rearing like a stock market crash or some form of imminent natural disaster.

To me, moms and dads should be measured and wise, not panicked and fretful. It takes a while—and a lot of scratched bumpers—to master that kind of parenting.

Or maybe parenting masters us?

##### * The daughter responds:
*My sister taught me always to call my dad after an accident. His moral support in those situations is one of his more appealing qualities.*

##### ** The columnist adds:
*An actual and common weekend routine.*

# SHE NEVER CALLS, SHE NEVER WRITES . . .

*February 21, 2015*

Dear Daughter,

We have not seen you for a while now, so I thought we might check in. Did you fall off the edge of the Earth? Were you smothered by one of those award show red carpets you used to work? Your mother worries, you know, and I am just curious. Well, I am more than curious. I feel abandoned.

Apparently you've dumped us for your career.

I can understand that, for you've always had a wonderful work ethic.

In fact, you are so dedicated, so efficient, so headed for big executive posts that friends have suggested paternity tests to locate your actual father. Let me end the suspense: Your real father is out there somewhere. And he is me.

Have you ever noticed the resemblance? We both talk too loud at parties and cry a little when we laugh too much at our own jokes. It is only with a mouthful of food that we ever achieve anything approaching mental clarity. We are both drawn to twinkly saloons and the kind of Formica-countered old dives where they quilt the burritos in tortillas the size of Sacramento.

How you ended up way out there in fancy Santa Monica is beyond me. Eating at one of the clangy restaurants there is like dining in the percussion section of a major orchestra. Only louder.

I went looking for you the other night, in some pretentious place on Main where the pizzas look like abstract art and taste of roofing materials. I sat there marveling at the menu—magnificently arcane and more overthought than a grad-school poem. The $14 glass of chardonnay was the exact temperature of blood.

"Hello, Domino's? This is an emergency!"

Look, obviously your long absence has flummoxed us. I was never exactly a Fulbright scholar to begin with, so any slight drop in acuity presents a significant concern. If your laptop ever caught the mumps, I am how it would perform.

As we go about our daily routines, your mother and I are distracted— both by your absence and our pride in your career in the after-market ticket biz. The other day, I entered my work password into the microwave, then stood there cursing it for not working. I was so off my game that I actually used that cholesterol-free mayo your mother insists on buying in an effort to drive me from the house.

Listen, a lot has happened since you've been away. Lincoln was shot. Taiwan split from China. We had two more children—a princess, now twenty-three; a boy badger, now twelve.

Worst of all, in a recent column, I misspelled the word *tuchis* and now may be banned from using Yiddish in any of my future manifests. I protested to an editor that Yiddish represents almost eighty percent of worthwhile exclamations. Without Yiddish, I am Taylor Swift.

So there's that.

Meanwhile, the mortgage is lost somewhere in cyberspace, the bank outsourcing it to some service that collects mortgages. They made that very clear, only they haven't told me where to now send the check, so the money sits in the account just laughing at me, daring me to spend it. So I did.

Yesterday I bought a very clean 2001 Camaro from an older woman who flirted with me about my blue eyes yet insisted only on cash. Off she went with the wad of mortgage money, leaving me with a car the color of Rodney Dangerfield.

Over this, your mother is not happy. She says it is the kind of muscle car driven by ex-cons when they case your house at 2 a.m. In response, I tell her it was the car of my dreams (when I was eighteen).

So that's where your long absence has left us. Not so bad, though we miss your roaring laughter . . . the way your cheeks flush when you eat Thai food. How you always march too hard into the house, like a Scotsman stomping snakes.

There is, in your absence, the lack of a certain gleeful irreverence.

Each evening, your mother now waits by the window the way she did when you used to step off the bus in first grade, your hair full of rubber bands.

Bet that drove you nuts even then, her running out on the porch like you'd just returned from a month-long journey to the moon.

Look, parents are not easy people.

But should the urge ever hit you, feel free to stop by some time. Our house is your house. Our hearts are yours too.

And your mother is still waiting by the window.

Love,

Dad

* The older daughter responds:
*The best part about the commentary we're getting to add to these articles is pointing out where there are ironies or inside jokes that the reader would never understand. In this particular case, my dad was with me at the pizza spot on Main—I'd just seen him that very same week when this article ran. I had a friend's mother tagging me on Facebook and old bosses emailing me to call my family or stop in to say hi. Of course, that made me chuckle, and yet he did make Santa Monica feel so far away. By the end of the article I was left in sentimental tears, wishing I did see them just a little more. Just a little.*

**The columnist adds:**
*Adult children really have no idea how much their parents miss them.
I wish I had called and visited my own parents more often.*

# FATHERS & SONS

# THE CRAP IN OUR CAR

*May 2, 2009*

We pull off to the school drop-off. A kid gets out, and here's what comes pouring out of our family car:

- ☞ a hockey stick
- ☞ $27.50 in pennies
- ☞ a lacrosse ball
- ☞ a box of tampons
- ☞ two ticket stubs from Hollywood Park
- ☞ a copy of *Sports Illustrated*
- ☞ a tube of hemorrhoid cream
- ☞ an old pregnancy test (flunked)
- ☞ fourteen Starbucks cups
- ☞ a baseball glove

I drive away, leaving all of it, except for the baseball glove, the only thing of value in a car full of crud. See, it's T-ball season, and we might need the glove.

The glove is what the little guy sits on when he gobbles treats after the game. The glove is what he uses as an extra hat when the sun gets too hot.

The glove can be a monster mask, a punching bag, a pillow, a pet. The mavericks on our little T-ball team—there are several—occasionally use their gloves to catch baseballs, but such occurrences are rare. On this team, any conventional occurrence is pretty rare.*

A week or two ago, we had a game during which a helicopter flew over. The entire game just stopped. The batter, I think he was in mid-swing, dropped the bat and joined his teammates as they gazed up in wonder.

"Look," one gasped as if just born. "A helicopter."

Big deal, a helicopter. But to them, it was almost biblical, as if God were descending from the clouds. It was revelation and science, all wrapped in one loud little moment. Like them, the copter made many annoying noises.

Then the game resumed, and the batter, Scribner, clubbed the ball from here to Toledo.

They have freckles like umlauts and little red mustaches from guzzling postgame juice. They behave almost like mini-men: They don't breathe when they eat, choosing instead to inhale their food, then grunt and gasp as a sign that they are finished.

You can't coach this kind of stuff. It just happens.

And you should see the way their pants fit, even worse than mine. They cinch their belts as high as possible, between the nipples and the neck. Meanwhile, the shirts reach to their knees, like cocktail dresses. Really, it's a wonder they can run at all.

By the way, you should see this Scribner kid hit. Remember the tear that Manny Ramirez went on after he joined the Dodgers last season? Peanuts compared to what Scribner is doing this year.

"At home, he's broken four windows," his mother explains.

After the last window, Mom and Dad instituted the Four Strikes Law and took away Tyler's baseballs. Poor lad couldn't help himself and resorted to swinging at rocks all day in the driveway.

Such dedication to the game has paid off. Now, when Scribner sees an actual baseball coming his way, his eyes get as big as Michelins, and he almost vomits with anticipation. Scribner is going to the bigs, I'm pretty sure. The call from Colletti could come any second.

In fact, the Muir-Chase Plumbing Dodgers are loaded with talent, and I'm not just talking about the moms.

You should see these mothers, though: glorious, loving, devoted. They are focused on their sons like no moms before them. They know it's an increasingly tough world, and they want these little guys to succeed.

To a six-year-old's mom, a bad play isn't just a bad play. It's a sign of his other deficiencies: his inability to focus, his reluctance to practice. One bad play, and they resign themselves to the possibility that the kid isn't going to Stanford after all.

But except for Coach Scott, we haven't given up on anybody on this team. We practice our hitting relentlessly and, over the course of the season, have recorded several impressive outs on defense.

In T-ball, a routine out at second is greeted with the response usually reserved for grand slams and Broadway openings.

On one play, I think I scored it 1-3-9-4-7-7-7-7-7, the ball ricocheted off my knee, hit our second baseman, Keaton, in the worst possible place, his glove, then rolled around the infield where the guys tried to pounce on it, as if chasing an escaped Pekingese at a busy airport. The play lasted about fifteen minutes and came to a halt only when the rolling ball threatened to knock over several morning mimosas along the first base line, at which point one of the moms laid out for the ball and prevented almost certain catastrophe.

You can't coach this stuff. It just happens.

* The little guy responds:
*I remember one time in T-ball when the ball got stuck on the brim of my cap. I couldn't find it. How is that possible?*

The columnist adds:
*Wish I had a video. The ball hung on his hat for five seconds. Even Einstein couldn't have explained it. Nor could he explain T-ball.*

# REACHING FOR THE SUN

*January 25, 2014*

The round-lobed sweetgum tree that I planted a few months ago appears to be tilting a little to the north, like a Russian skyscraper or a knobby-kneed college center. I fear it may never right itself. It will only grow taller and more obviously wrong.

So it is with sons. Can you right them once they've rooted? Can dads and sons right each other?

With fathers, you sort of get what you get. No one ever gets to choose his old man.

If you did, you'd never pick a dad who plants crooked trees or eats oysters like nachos and prefers brats boiled in beer.

As an old-school American male, I am ornery one moment and wry the next. I yammer at traffic. I curse the TV, especially when quarterback Peyton Manning appears, trying to convince us that he actually drives a Buick. It blends my natural animosity toward other drivers with my paranoia over being hoodwinked.

The rest of the time I'm pretty content, ranting over the follies of the world but in silly-funny ways, and weekly for the past fifteen years, in a column that's distributed halfway to the moon. Can't be easy being the son of a man like that.

No, you don't get to pick your father.

Or your sons.

My younger son, only eleven, is still at that easy-breezy age. He looks at me and sees Zeus. He thinks I sublet the stars, control the tides, invented

Velcro and whipped cream.

With each new day, a fifth grader fills more of the world. He'll add muscles between breakfast and lunch. I see him now stretched out on the couch he outgrew this afternoon, taller than he was five breaths before.

Dear gawd, make all children as easy as an eleven-year-old. A life without caution or care. When he gets unhappy, I buy him a Slurpee.

For years, the Little Guy has been a main player in the column, replacing his older brother, the Boy, who sort of aged out of that slapstick suburban world. He'd grown older, and more testy. He disappeared only in print. In my life, he was a constant. A joy some days. Some days not. Tall, handsome, and a handful.

We got along lousy for a while. Now we get along better, and, eventually, we will get along great. Because that's what guys do, persevere around the tripwires of passive-aggressive paternal love. Until both—son and father—grow up a little more.

As with most men, we are better/happier when we're doing things. Last summer, we took a long, grinding hike through the mountains, two agonizing days when he bounded up a 9,000-foot chunk of Sierra granite as if it were merely a ten-inch-high pitching mound.

I loped behind, an aging Lawrence of Arabia. Fleas clung to me. Horseflies gnawed my ears. Aphids ate my AARP card.

It was perfect.*

With jaunts like these, I show that I love him. Only rarely do I come right out and say those words. Maybe you can, maybe your old man could. I'm not that guy.

To me, it seems too touchy-feely. It would also jeopardize the easy and irreverent camaraderie we've finally established.

Admittedly, closing emotional distance is a good thing, but were I to suddenly sit my twenty-eight-year-old son down tomorrow to tell him point blank: "Love you, dude. Love the way you're turning out. Proud of the man you're becoming," I might get laughed off the couch. He'd look at me blankly, waiting for the punch line.

We've got some work left to do, he and I. I fear for his future, his livelihood, the challenges he faces from a less-benevolent world that no longer values loyalty or teamwork. I think he should do more. He thinks I could do more to help. The truth teeters somewhere in between. But I love him unconditionally. Some men can say that. Some can't.

So in lieu of those words, I show my feelings with random little gestures. By taking him camping. By talking curveballs. Or sharing photos, of aspens full with fall, those butterscotch bombshells of the Eastern Sierra.

Crooked trees that eventually righted themselves.

Like fathers. Like sons.

* **The older boy responds:**
*Taking a trip like that with the man who instilled a passion in me for all things outdoors is something I will truly remember forever. It's with good reason that climbing a mountain is a metaphor for all other endeavors in life.*

**The columnist responds:**
*Exactly.*

# SAY HELLO TO GRACE KELLY

*July 2, 2016*

On a lazy morning at the library, we discovered that you can check out an astounding fifty items at once, which pretty much should cover us for the rest of the summer—an item a day, a novel, a biography, a classic Jimmy Stewart flick.

While picking out DVDs, I talked the little guy into *Rear Window*, the Hitchcock masterpiece. Not only had he never heard of the movie, he'd never heard of Hitchcock. When Grace Kelly first enters Stewart's cramped apartment—like gold plate, like plasma jets off the summer sun—he audibly gasps.

"Say hello to Grace Kelly," I say.

"Who?" he asks.

"Grace Kelly."

An evening breeze went right out of him.

He is transitioning, from boyhood to something else—we're not entirely sure what. The anti-puberty paint we purchased for his bedroom appears not to be working. The other day he was scolded for scratching at his bare stomach too close to a bowl of steaming green beans.

The guy's got a ways to go is what I'm saying. We all do. The male of this species will always be an unfinished house, minus a few shingles. That accounts for some of our charm and much of the aggravation we sometimes cause. Each day I wake up, I'm relieved my mate of 300 years didn't smother me in my sleep.

Meanwhile, the boy is a spec house with a lot of unfinished surfaces.

His edges need some serious sanding. At thirteen, he will still sit through a movie where the dogs lip-synch the dialogue or talking chipmunks oversell the jokes. He has been raised on this, as well as a steady diet of bombs and exploding cities.

Sure, those will always be our very best movies, but lately the little guy has shown a burgeoning interest in movies with more of a soul.

So after visiting the library, we sat on the couch and watched *Rear Window*. In it, a keen-eyed photographer, housebound with a broken leg, determines that a neighbor has killed his nagging wife. Simple, right? You could've shot it with your iPhone. You could fit the plot points on the back of your Starbucks cup.

Sinister and sweaty, it was the perfect movie for a summer night.* As it opens, New York City is suffering a heat wave. Neighbors never interact, until something goes terribly wrong, then they wail at one another. In that sense, it was very much like the New York of today.

Now, I don't know much about movies, or life, or death, or anything for that matter. The Baldwin brothers all look the same to me, and I can't tell Nancy O'Dell from Deborah Norville. These days, I can barely even tell a Camry from an Accord. The world seems to be suffering—and a little dead—from sensible sedans and their human equivalents.

But this much I am sure of: Good scripts are literature. Like books, good movies help to make us interesting adults. And great movies all have great endings.

That's the big note—the great endings. You can have a terrific career that ends poorly. You can even have a wonderful romance that fizzles in the end. But you will never ever, ever, ever, ever, ever write, produce, or witness a great movie that doesn't have an amazing ending.

Paul Newman had the best take on this. When told that the first pages of a script were the most critical, he agreed, but insisted that the last minutes of a movie were what mattered most of all. *Chinatown*.

*The Wizard of Oz. Casablanca. E.T. Good Will Hunting.* All end with surprise, another element to world-class storytelling.

So, there you have my theory on movies.

Here's my theory on little boys:

They take a while. They dream, they play, they waste a lot of time. They screw up, and find joy in screwing up, so they screw up some more. In no way are they sensible sedans.

At one time, their lingering little-boy temperaments were perfectly suited to jumping on a sailing ship, or a horse, and hitting horizons that scared the bejesus out of everybody else. After six million years of human evolution, little boys have been preprogrammed to take on a world that hardly exists anymore.

Now they sit on beds and couches, destroying kingdoms with their thumbs in video games that are about as compelling to me as talking dogs.

But boys can still have terrific endings — at least most of them will.

I know. I used to be one.


**\* The little guy adds:**
*I remember screaming like a girl during this movie.*

**The columnist responds:**
*No, you screamed like a fire siren.*

# THE BOYS OF SUMMER

*April 16, 2011*

Seems to me great athletes have a sort of rhythm to their trot, and the Little Giants of the eight-year-old division are no exception. They bossa nova to first, they samba into second, they giggle-sing into third. After the practice where we taught them the proper way to slide, they stayed late, skimming across the cardboard appliance box as if taking an escalator to the moon.

"Time to go," I finally had to say.

"My mom's from Boston," one of them tells me.

"So?"

"So that's where she's from," he says with a shrug.

Obviously, a ball field is a tough place to have a meaningful conversation, and the sooner the Little Giants learn this, the more prepared for life they will be. Meaningful conversation never got anyone anywhere. I know that from working in a newsroom. Several times, just on a lark, I've tried to engage in meaningful conversation. The other parties just looked at me kind of crooked.

"Huh?"

"Never mind," I said.

And that was the end of that.

So it is in a dugout, where they pass the time between at-bats with discussions of bugs, bulldogs, and the ten coolest things you can do with a dead lizard.

One of the guys—my own son, my own pre-caffeinated DNA—

removed a Band-Aid the other day that he claimed to have worn "for three entire years." No one could prove otherwise. His poor mother—the one with the eyes of a hostage—just shrugged.

"Could be," she said, and went back to texting her bartender.

Three years with the same Band-Aid? The little guy's teammates really liked that. Three years?

On the Giants, we value commitment. I'm all the time telling them that we function best as a team, not eleven individuals. One unit. Under God. Indivisible. With liberty and juice boxes for all.

"Remember, there's no *i* in team," I tell them.

"There's not?"

"Yes, there is."

"*T-I-E-A* . . ."

"Trust me, there's no *i*," I say.

"There should be," says Rabbit.

"*T-I-E-I-O* . . ."

How close is this team? I claimed them all on my taxes. No biggie. I now list 239 dependents, from all the teams I've ever coached.

But it has been a great season for the Little Giants, and I think that's what the IRS will judge us on. As usual, we gave all the players nicknames. To reflect their identities, we mostly stuck with swamp creatures. Or superheroes.

"The moms have nicknames, too," I tell the parents.

"We do?" squeaks Squeaky.

"But we can't tell you," I say.

Okay, maybe we'll reveal them at the year-end team party. This year, we're having ours in Vegas. Gator said he knows someone who knows someone who might get us into the Tropicana. Fingers crossed.

However we celebrate it, it will be a road trip to remember.

Just in case, I secured a bond to guarantee against damage. Seemed the sensible thing. On the Little Giants, we are all about sensible behavior.

We are also quite delusional—most men are—a mixture of sensible and delusional, one following the other in emotional lockstep. We also have no real sense of scope.

When we played the Red Sox a couple of weeks ago, one of the boys thought we were playing the real Red Sox. Ortiz and such.

"We should be so lucky," I said.

"Hey, coach, where's right field?" someone asked.

By the way, in twenty years of this, I've concluded that there is nothing quite so unfair as the way a ball comes off the bat in a Little League game. It defies physics, gravity, the laws of rotation. Like something Lewis Carroll wrote.

Yes, hovering over a Little League field are these black holes that make a baseball behave pretty badly. Plus, you could chop an onion in the time it takes the ball to go from the pitcher's fingers to the catcher's glove. A lot of paranormal mischief can happen in that time, including the batter's beer pong swing.

I watch through my fingers, as if witnessing an exorcism.

All ball fields are a little haunted, but these cursed forces are most apparent on a Little League diamond. A sure pop out will fall like a teardrop between three infielders, who were so close at the time that they might've been swapping gum, or switching Band-Aids, or having a spitting contest. Eight-year-old boys might be the most social creatures ever.

"All my teeth are loose," says one.

"Today at school, I glued a tooth back in," says another.

"That's so silarious," says the third.

What's "silarious"? Apparently, it's a combo of "silly" and "hilarious." You know, silarious.

Yes, busy as they are, the Little Giants of the eight-year-old league still find time to improve the English language. Little Giants. Little Shakespeares.

Constant as the northern star.

# WHAT A MOTHER, NATURE IS

*June 14, 2013*

Oy, camping!

My backpack is the size of a Honda Fit. It has fifty-four pockets, twenty-seven zippers, and a functioning spleen. It weighs as much as a nine-by-twelve rug with a dead Soprano rolled up inside. To shed it at the end of a long hike is the sweetest thing imaginable.

We have backpacked eight miles into the wilderness, no world record but nothing to sneeze at either, eight miles straight up a broken escalator. Eight miles from the nearest bucket of ice or cheeseburger, medium rare. Me, I get too far from cheeseburgers, and I start to panic a little, my breath coming in short, troubled bursts.

This isn't a vacation; it's a John Denver song.

I hate John Denver.

And now we're at this remote campsite, the most perfect spot you could ever imagine.*

The ponderosa pine? God's whiskers. The trout in a nearby stream? So wild, so refreshingly stupid, they'll almost jump in your pocket.

I was just asking myself, "Could this possibly get any better?" when it starts to rain. Hello, front desk? Please send up a hotel room.

Oh, and then I find out I have to dig my own latrine.

Oy, camping!

But after the first day, we see no one, and when isn't that a blessing? Time slows. Smartphones go dumb. We chop firewood. Burn firewood. Chop some more.

Chopping wood warms you twice, someone once said. When you cut it, and again when it burns.

Love this time of year. The way beer caps ting around my pants pockets with the car keys. The way dusk goes on and on and on.

And this backpacking trip is summer amplified, a five-hour hike straight up into the sky near June Lake, north of Mammoth.

By the time we arrive, there is a heat in my hips that I have never experienced, and my hamstrings are barking to go out.

And then I get to set up the two-person rental tent.

To see me set up a two-person rental tent for the first time is to witness a type of performance art rarely experienced outside New York or London. It's like watching a drunk get kicking mad at his $7 beach chair.

"There, that's it," I finally say.

"Dad, don't think so," says my son.

I try again. This time, a pirate ship.**

Fortunately, there are only 400 possible combinations of tent stakes and Chinese nylon. Eventually, I assemble something resembling a two-man tent. It's a gift, really.

As is this three-day backpacking trip—my older son's idea.

After we pulled into the parking lot earlier in the day, he took off down Rush Creek Trail like a fighter jet. I followed, zigzagging up the side of this granite and slate Matterhorn with a forty-pound pack on my sweaty shoulders. Hey wait, hey wait.

My son supplies the route, packs the bear canister full of freeze-dried food.

Let me tell you, nothing enhances the flavor in food like freeze-drying it. The beef stew I have for dinner tastes like warm, shredded Levi's.

And determined to pack light, we forgo certain delicacies: morning coffee, an evening cigar. We also wish we'd brought a book or two. And a couple of beers to plop in the remaining patches of snow.

But it is the fireside cigar I miss most on this little trip.

Normally a rich man's endeavor, smoking a cigar while fishing or camping is one of life's great small joys, two great flavors of braided smoke.

"Wish I had a cigar," I say.

"Dad, I think your shoe's burning," says my son.

Turns out chopping wood warms you thrice.

As darkness rolls in, so do thoughts of what's out there. *Is the bear canister far enough away? Who left those carbine cartridges under a nearby rock? Is that a mule deer crashing through the shrubs or something more menacing?*

Da bears?

I shake my flashlight at the shadows. It's the kind of flashlight that you have to rattle a few times to get to work—shake, shake, shake. What's with that? Shake, shake, shake. We can take the gluten out of a potato chip, the caffeine out of coffee, but we still can't make a flashlight with a light in it.

What a mother, nature.

Who needs it, right?

We all do.

* **The older boy responds:**
*This was the type of secluded paradise that for some reason almost makes you feel guilty.*

** **The older boy adds:**
*It was at that exact moment I realized why my old man wasn't an engineer.*

**The columnist adds:**
*I'm barely a writer! This was, though, one of the great trips of all time. I'd do it again, but not sure I could get up the hill.*

# A FEW FAVORITES

# THE CHICKEN CHILI RECIPE

*November 5, 2011*

So I'm spooning with the dog again, and every couple of minutes he spasms in his sleep, a sort of esophageal quake-quiver. I don't know if he's worried about work or having sex dreams. There's the blue-eyed Akita next door—as dogs go, a real looker—and I think we're all a little smitten with her.

Anyway, that's how Halloween started at our house. Sure, it was a little scary, but thrilling, too.

I'm about to enter Snickers rehab at the new Betty Ford Clinic where they treat candy disorders, but before I go, I want to brief you on how the holiday went. Halloween remains my favorite, largely because it doesn't involve gifts. Plus, you can slay zombies.*

Halloween is also the little guy's favorite. He apparently believes it's the night baby Jesus was born, a cross-pollination of holidays that happens with young children. I didn't want to crush his little spirit, so I just went with that. But it was a little awkward when, at the first house we visited on Halloween, he started caroling.

For tricks-or-treats, we went to a neighboring neighborhood where the yards look like Hollywood sets and they give out candy the size of small pets.

The kids travel in swarms, sort of like a ground fog, down the streets and up the walks, the escorting parents worried about losing them. Can you imagine returning home after Halloween with one fewer kid than you left with? Or worse, one extra?

Every once in a while, one of the trick-or-treaters goes stumbling over some flagstone steps, and some of the Chardonnay Moms, too. Loss of motor control is apparently one of the side effects of chardonnay, along with dizziness, slurred speech, and table dancing.

By the way, another dad was asking about Chardonnay Moms the other day, what distinguishes them from their predecessors (Soccer Moms), and I explained that the Chardonnay Moms tend to be fortysomething fitness freaks with the fat content of pencils.

For example, when you hold a Chardonnay Mom against a light, as you would a glass of white wine, you can visually make out her skeleton. And if she happens to have recently swallowed a key, or has a filling or any piercings, you can make them out, too—in silhouette.

These moms also, occasionally, can be seen hoisting a glass of chardonnay at the many school fundraisers they attend. Veni! Vidi! Sippi!

So, onward we go, stumbling toward the holidays as if pursuing some sort of prize. November might be my favorite month, with its oxblood evening skies, the way the autumn moon slips behind the clouds, the smell of the neighbor's septic system backing up into the pool.

We still have some pumpkin seeds left over; my wife, Posh, salts them and roasts them in the oven, and we chew-chew-chew them till they're almost soft enough to eat, then swallow them anyway.

And, for the first time this fall, Posh made a batch of her sensational chicken chili. I know what you're thinking: chicken chili, how un-American. Trust me, after you've sampled Posh's chicken chili, you might quit the other stuff.**

Let me walk you through it:

First, you kill a chicken, or if you're pressed for time, buy one at the deli, where a whole roasted chicken often sells for $5. An uncooked chicken is more. That's America. No, I am not taking questions.

In a big pot, sauté two tablespoons of chopped garlic and a medium chopped onion in oil, add the peeled chicken and three jars of Trader

Joe's salsa verde—so now not only is it chicken chili, it's *green* chicken chili. Stay with me.

You slosh it around a while, maybe an hour, add a couple of cans of cannellini beans and a tablespoon of cumin, a spice that tastes lousy till you add it to food. Oh, and a cup or two of chicken broth.

Then slosh it around some more.

Serve with a scoop of sour cream and a dash of hot sauce. It feeds six normal adults. Or about sixty Chardonnay Moms.

If it's not the best chili ever, if it doesn't change your life in substantial ways, clear your skin, vanquish any rashes, straighten your teeth, improve your sex life, rejuvenate your mortal soul, Posh will give you your money back.

For this is not just chili; it's more of a supremely delicious elixir. My only fear is that I may be underselling it.

Please keep in mind that Posh has no money, so she'll probably reimburse you in wine corks, which is how I get my allowance these days.

Bon appétit. Bon November.

**Posh responds:**
*\* Chris loves Halloween because he can raid the little guy's candy stash.*

*\*\* He always gives me credit for this. Truth is, this chili recipe actually comes courtesy of the lovely and patient older daughter. And I think she stole it, too.*

# THE BRIDE WITH THE LEMONADE HAIR

*July 22, 2004*

The bride is wearing a beautiful white gown. We all know what white represents. That's right: surrender.

"You must become a student of your wife, Andrew," the minister is saying. "Anticipate her wants and desires, before she even voices them herself."

Now they tell me. In fact, had someone mentioned this at my own wedding, it would've saved me a lot of agony. When it comes to marriage, I almost never study. I've still got homework due from 1984.

The minister continues. A car alarm goes off, interrupting his next bit of advice.

"Andrew, that's the Lord's way of saying, 'Listen up,'" the minister says.

I have been to a lot of weddings, perhaps too many. After college, there was a flurry of them. Who knows why exactly? I'm pretty sure we were brainwashed by our mothers. But believe me, a lot of those brains needed washing.

Back then, the receptions were like the closing ceremonies of childhood. Too much beer. Too much cake. Almost every weekend, another college buddy fell. Until there were no more buddies. Saturday nights have been pretty quiet ever since.

Two decades later, it is our children who are beginning to tie the knot. J.P. and Nancy, the neighbors down the block, are marrying off their eldest daughter, the one with the lemonade hair. The one who was just twelve. You mean she's finished grade school? What do you mean she's done with college?

But for one afternoon, time seems to stop. By the ocean's edge we gather—handsome Californians in linen and cotton and splotchy summer tans. A backdrop of blue. You can hardly tell where the sky ends and the ocean takes over.

And then there's that sea air. The breath of angels, this air. Nice job, God. For a single guy, you sure throw a nice wedding.*

"Do you, Summer, take Andrew to cherish and to hold, till death do you part?" the minister asks.

"I do," she says.

Of course, she does. Only in Julia Roberts movies do brides back out at moments like this. Because in real life, the crowd would kill you. Everyone got all dressed up for nothing?

None of that drama here. It's a near-perfect ceremony in someone's near-perfect yard. The bride's brother leads a hymn. The minister elicits some light laughter. I'm a big believer in short weddings and long marriages.

The couple exchanges the two rings. We all know what that symbolizes. Little handcuffs.

"Ladies and gentlemen," the young minister says, "I now present to you Andrew and Summer."

I'll tell you this about marriage. I still get chills at moments like this. Because, day in and day out, our own union has been an unabashed orgy of love, passion, and emotional intimacy. Christmas we take off, but every other day my wife and I have all those things. Obviously, it can be physically exhausting. It's amazing we both don't weigh, like, eleven pounds.

"Look at all the food," the little girl gasps inside the nearby reception tent.

"Finally," I say.

"Please don't embarrass us," my lovely bride says.

She's seen me at buffets before. She knows the dangers. By virtue of a cold and tiny heart, I am able to fit more free food inside my body than almost any other man. My motion with a fork resembles a racquetball serve.

"Did you taste these shrimp?" I ask my wife.

"How can you eat so much?" she wonders, with breathless disbelief.

"One big bite at a time," I explain through a wad of beef kebab.

Later, she warns me off dessert.

"They're very rich," she says.

"Really?" I say.

"Yes," she says, "you may only want three."**

Fortunately, I have a baby to chase around. He toddles from one table to another, locking eyes with any eligible woman under the age of 110.

He may be the next Brando, this baby. He doesn't talk so much as grunt and stumble around with an unexplainable charisma. Every time I look up, he's tunneling under some lovely stranger's dress.

"Where's your dignity?" I ask him at one point.

"Left it in the car," he says.

From table to table, he goes. He shows up, smiles, then goes right for the prettiest face. He favors the older ones, age ten and up.

"You can't let him go like that," my wife says.

"I'll catch him," the little girl offers.

"Try to keep him off the cake," I say.

I have been to a hundred weddings. Most of the marriages lasted, some didn't. But I'll say this: I never lose faith. I never stop believing that it's the front-end of the rainbow.

For a thousand years from now, there may be no more oil. No more *Survivor* episodes. Even Ralph Nader may be gone. But one thing won't have changed. Human beings will still have weddings. Of all the mammals, we are probably the most hopelessly romantic.

Today, the young teacher with the lemonade hair is marrying the handsome future cop. Think there's a future there?

I do.

**The columnist adds:**
*\* If I am remembered for one line, let it be this one:*
*"Nice job, God. For a single guy, you sure throw a nice wedding."*

*\*\* But she's the funny one, obviously.*

# A WARM POSH ON A COOL DAY

*October 11, 2008*

It's raining steadily—in the key of B-flat—the drops pinging against the windows and burping down the downspouts. Honestly, I don't know how much more of this winter weather I can take.

"What's that sound?" the little guy asks.

"A nor'easter," I say.

"Dad, we live in LA," says the little girl.

"We do?"

Love the rain. Without fail, the first real rain of the year comes just after I clean the skylight or wash both cars. For dads with a God complex—and that's more than a few—washing the skylight is a surefire way to take complete control of the nation's weather systems.

"I think," says Posh, with a shiver, "that I'll put a fire in the fireplace."

Spreads heat everywhere she goes, that woman. Bad enough she's started wearing sweaters again, in broad daylight, with children around.

She's my Bond girl. My muse. My very best pal. When she puts on a sweater and starts a fire in the fireplace, it's almost more romance than I can accommodate.

"What do you want for dinner?" she asks.

Yarn. That sweater. You.

"How 'bout hamburgers?" Posh purrs.

"I was going to say that," I say.

Or, we could go down to the local Oktoberfest, if this crummy weather ever lets up. I swear, I've been stuck in the house now for almost two hours.

Naturally, I'm starting to go a little stir-crazy. I have Miss October romping around in her Gap sweater, lighting fires she can't put out. And I've got the little guy draped over my shoulders like a human scarf, begging me—puleeeeeease?—to roughhouse.

You might not realize this—or maybe you do—but about half the time I write, I either have a kid on my lap or another kid with his hand in my pocket, frisking me for cash. Does it show up in the writing? I'm sure you had the vague sense that something was a little off. Well, that's just part of it.

The other day, I starting thinking I might have this West Nile virus.* Or, in my case, Midwest Nile virus, a high fever and deep lethargy that comes from following the Cubs for almost half a century.

Every five years, along comes another malady that has to do with Americans being fatigued. For a while, everyone had Epstein-Barr, which was similar but not the same as Lyme disease (yeah, right, a deer tick turned you into Sleeping Beauty).

Now it's West Nile we're supposed to worry about, and, frankly, I suspect that the drug companies are all behind this somehow, creating "diseases" for what is really just a chronic and common condition: getting older.

It doesn't help that every year, our days start earlier and last longer. Or that the family home—our refuge, our Fort Apache—seems more vulnerable than ever before.

Lately, when Posh walks past, she either yawns or sighs, sometimes both. Me, if I were any more nocturnal, I'd be a raccoon.**

But that's okay. I don't need any help counting my blessings. I've got ten fingers and ten or more toes, and that human scarf across my shoulders has a bunch more.

It's October, after all, and we are rich with playoff games and the lush sounds of marching bands. They're offering bratwurst omelets down at the local diner and beer by the bootful at the nearby street fair (make mine a double).

We are blessed, too, to have gotten our soccer match in today, beating the rain by only a couple of hours. As every parent of a five-year-old knows, if you don't "run the children" daily, they become cranky and a threat to the very house they live in. Big termites.

Our soccer team today was extra-frisky, turbo-charged by the fall chill. It was forty degrees cooler than the week before, and all the moms were wearing sweaters, which I'll confess made it tough to concentrate on my little team's latest game plan: total domination.

Unfortunately, our opponents (the Blue Sharks) had the same game plan: total domination. It was a tight tussle—back and forth, forth and back, to and fro.

Thing is, five-year-olds have no idea when a soccer game actually begins or ends. For them, the contest starts the second their little shoes hit the scraggly turf.

Today, they ran before the ref blew the whistle and after he blew the whistle and for thirty minutes after the game ended. Like little retrievers, they ran and ran, celebrating the wonderful fall air, with an energy level their parents can only envy and admire.

I say go for it, you little princes. Run like a raindrop.

For soon enough you'll be tired, too, just like us. I give you thirty to forty years, max.


**Posh responds:**
* *West Nile? That explains it all now.*
** *Only nocturnal if you base it on East Coast time. He's roadkill by ten, usually.*

# FRIDAY NIGHT LIGHTS

*November 1, 2008*

We're sitting in a heap of people, right in the middle of the bleachers, under the Friday night lights. Generally, I don't like being in a heap of people. But this is special—homecoming—and I am surrounded by some of the nicest people I know.

"Seriously, do you ever wish you were seventeen again?" I ask, looking around at all the bright-eyed kids.

"Just watch the game, okay?" someone answers.

Actually, I have a lot in common with teenagers. Like them, my body is changing in new and mysterious ways. Like them, I have feelings I really can't express.

Plus, like a teenager, I am hopeful about the future, almost relentlessly optimistic that things will work out, even in tough times like these.

In fact, I have a schoolboy crush on all of humanity, especially the female ones, of which there are many in these high school bleachers, including the hottie sitting next to me.

"Wanna go to the dance with me?" I ask my wife.

"Just watch the game," Posh says again.

"Wanna go to the dance with me?" I ask the little guy.

"Sure," he squeaks.

Admission to this game was a little steep—six bucks—and the closest parking spot must've been a mile away. They raised the price of a burger and a drink ($5), and the stands have no seat backs or cup holders. By gawd, there aren't even any corporate suites.

Yet, I still believe a high school football game is the last great sports deal on the planet. For one thing, you're among people you've known and liked and loved for years, since these seniors were in kindergarten, in fact. Sure, there are a few of them you maybe don't like. But like high school itself, by the time it's almost over like this, people have more or less made amends.

"I've got a book I want you to read," I tell my buddy Rhymer.

"He doesn't know how to read," someone next to him says.

"I'll read it to him," I say.

At halftime, the leggy dentist and her quiet husband show up. In the third quarter, our five-year-old loses a tooth, the little guy's eyes watering up under the stadium lights as if he just scored the winning touchdown. In the fourth quarter, someone whispers an inappropriate story; either Bill or Jeff.

I've been to bigger and more expensive venues, glitzy and glamorous, celebrities all around. Rose Bowl. Staples. Disney Hall.

But give me a high school homecoming game any day, on a Friday evening just cool enough for a sweater, the entire weekend beckoning.

"You got vodka in that water bottle?" I ask Rhymer, who answers by telling me a long story about this tavern in New York that won't even sell vodka because the proprietor considers it an inferior, tasteless drink.

So, anyway, I'm pretty sure there is vodka in the water bottle, though I have no proof other than the sneaking suspicion that I'm the only adult in these bleachers who is actually sober. Had I not come directly from work, I might've had a little nip first as well, for it's homecoming, the little girl's last as a high school student. In the fall air, there is the misty cocktail of something drawing to a close.

That feeling continues the next night, when parents and teenagers gather at a luscious house in the hills to see the kids off to the homecoming dance. In fifteen minutes, fifty or so teenagers will board a rental bus and head off to a pre-dance dinner, but not before the parents snap off a zillion photos. The digital cameras chatter like machine guns. Someone notes how the boys are finally taller than the girls.

"Our last homecoming," Meghan's mom says wistfully.

Known these parents for at least twelve years, many of them. We went on field trips together, staged school fairs, joked our way through Indian Princesses and Scouts, soccer, divorces, and childbirth.

Bruce, one of my favorites, coached alongside me during our glory years of AYSO, his skinny, pretzel-legged daughter one of my star forwards.

"Marisa, shoot the ball!" I can still hear Bruce screaming. "Shoot the stinkin' ball!"

Suddenly, Marisa is seventeen and wearing heels and little dabs of silver on the inside corners of her eyes. Marisa is probably too dazzling and full of life for our little suburb and must move on soon—to Berkeley, or New Haven, or Palo Alto, places better suited to dazzling teenagers like her and the little girl.

Seriously, would you like to be seventeen again?

No. But I wouldn't mind being thirty-eight again and doing this all again. For in the suburbs, the good stuff goes by too quickly. Now it's the fourth quarter, the final play, the ultimate Hail Mary.

Marisa, shoot the ball.

# THE SCHOOL CARNIVAL

*May 29, 2010*

Gophers are devouring the front yard, the little pests everywhere. I'm thinking of trapping them full-time and developing a line of gopher gloves, mittens, and sun bonnets that I'll market on the Web, with proceeds going directly to me. I'm sick of all these charitable causes.

And I'm tired of drinking domestic beer at every breakfast. For the next fifty years, I want to drink German and drive German, though I'll confess that I find the Bavarians to be a little weak when it comes to air-conditioning. You'll usually do better with a GM car in that regard. Trust me, I've studied it. The Germans just don't do AC well. If you want well-engineered air-conditioning, hire some hayseed from Alabama. Give him a protractor and a bottle of Jack Daniel's and stand back. Cool things come to those who wait.

To paraphrase Coleridge, summer is setting in with its usual severity, leaving us all a little edgy. In particular, the gophers have gone wild, and there is little reason to think they won't take the house and the cars before they are done.

These, of course, are the famed thirty-year gophers, renowned for the devastation they cause. The other day, while out running, I paused with several other residents to watch a gopher pop its head out of a hole in some green space along the boulevard. Such is the level of sophistication in the place where I reside.

"I can't believe we're standing here watching a gopher," one of the spectators finally said.

Me, I couldn't believe more people hadn't joined us. In our town, you could organize entire festivals around such events. And let me just note there is nothing boring about watching a little rodent trying to determine whether it is safe to leave his little subterranean condo and venture forth into one of the nicer LA suburbs at midday when everybody is out.

Little pal, let me just say this: It is never safe, nor is it sane. At least wait till happy hour, when folks are a little less frantic.

Speaking of the sauce, I have never seen so many sober moms in one place as at the end-of-the-year school carnival the other day—a frightening and unexpected sight. Usually, to assemble a gaggle of women of this caliber, you need to be serving adult drinks. Some of these women haven't had a beverage in years that didn't have a salted rim. Others wear wine on their lips like Chanel. When you kiss them hello, it's like kissing Tuscany full on the mouth. Bottoms up. Yum.

Listen, I'm not being judgmental, for the warmer months are upon us, and doctors say it's important to keep your fluids up.

Not this day, though. The school carnival is a major event, and no one was prepared to face it with anything but their full wits about them. There must've been a half-dozen bouncy houses on the school grounds, and you would not have believed the cake walk—I should've taken pictures. For five hours, they gave away cake after cake, and when it was over, they gave away more cake. It was like the glory days of Florence.

The carnival took place on the perfect day in the perfect place; everybody said so. I have never seen quite so idyllic a venue as an elementary school in May. The flowers, they're chronic, and the songbirds flit about as if about to make love, which they probably are.

There were beautiful moms and beautiful kids and fathers shaped like piggy banks. Pretty much the American dream.

In one tiny glitch, they had my wife, Posh, working the ticket booth, which is where most of the money changes hands. I love Posh for a million reasons, but not for the way she handles financial transactions. Thirty years later, we are still paying off our wedding, for example.

It was a good investment: The union gifted us with two adorable, appreciative kids (and two others as well). But our wedding probably could've done without the three pianists in Liberace suits and twelve accordion players. Though it seemed tasteful at the time, it was more than we could afford. Then again, how do you put a price on a fairy tale?

By the way, this just in: *The Wall Street Journal* said that the reason fixed-rate home mortgages have sunk so low is that European investors are looking to sock away funds in the US after the recent calamity in Greece.

Hence, they are pouring money into long-term mortgages, which, as we know from the events of the past couple of years, is an absolutely foolproof place to invest your money. Never has there been the hint of scandal or instability there. In my book, that's just smart investing.

Yikes.

Hey, it's not my world. I just live here.

# STUCK BETWEEN SANITY & SUBURBIA

*October 15, 2011*

For me, exasperation is a form of exercise. You should've seen me at the soccer game Saturday, big gasping breaths as if drowning. I recommend it to anyone looking to lose a few pounds while tiptoeing the fine line between sanity and suburbia.

"You look like you've lost weight," our friend Barbara said after the game.

"I'm mostly wasting away," I explained.

"You look good," she said.

Thanks.

The team performed well, except that in the second quarter I realized that my players seemed unable to run sideways. They performed only forward and back, a broken waltz.

One defender, propelled by an attack of gas, actually left the earth during a clearing kick. Again, he did not move laterally, only forward. We're going to work on that Thursday in practice, this technique of moving side to side. Naturally, we'd like to use our gas attacks as effectively as possible.

Speaking of exasperation, another good source of this is college kids.

The other day, I did a very brave thing: I had an opinion. I even voiced it,* which is really going out on a limb in our house. Personally, I'd rather tumble off the roof than argue with another female.

The issue: Who was paying for the college girl's weekend trip, where word had it she and a couple of her sorority types were shacking up in some fancy Chicago hotel?

So, I politely inquired, "WHO IN GOD'S NAME IS PAYING FOR ALL THIS?!!" knowing full well that I was, but, you know, just asking because I love to see their pupils dilate when they're lying.**

We seem so clueless sometimes, dads do, so beaten down by children and the fickleness of this year's NFL outcomes. (My bookie won't even return my emails.) But a lot of dads are paying more attention than is generally believed.

"Hey, do you know who's paying for all this?" my buddy Eugene asks over the phone.

Eugene's daughter is also going, the beautiful and quiet Quinn. But as we all know, still blondes run deep.

I've experienced some scary things in my life—car crashes, natural disasters, William Shatner singing. But nothing prepares you for autumn in the suburbs.

There is a pile of costumes on a chair in the living room, meaning that either Halloween is approaching or someone is planning a major bank heist. Secretly, I'm hoping for the heist.

"Um, ouch."

"What, Dad?" says Darth Vader.

"Why did you clunk me with your lightsaber?" I ask.

"I really can't see that good," Darth Vader explains from behind the heavy mask.

Notice that there is no "sorry" in his answer. I guess when you're Darth Vader, you don't need to apologize. You just plow through life, clunking things with your lightsaber.

So the little guy is trying out the pile of costumes that the leggy dentist dropped off, her son having outgrown them. The little guy is in Halloween heaven, trying out a Superman, a cowboy, a ninja, a Peter Pan.

"One Peter Pan per house, please," my wife, Posh, announces.

Hysterical, huh? The bludgeoning implication is that I'm some sort of Peter Pan, just because I still wear Scooby-Doo underwear—not every night, but enough.

In fact, I've come to terms with middle age. It really is the greatest age of all.

Last weekend, just to remind ourselves of where we are in life, a bunch of the other dads and I played our traditional touch football season opener. You know, just to pinpoint the places where we're really old.

I mean, we all know our knees aren't what they used to be, but to determine exactly where the arthritis is settling in, there's nothing like running up and down a field at three-quarter speed with a bunch of other dunderheads. Like the soccer players, we tend not to move laterally. Poor Matt: On the third play—while trying to blast free of a defender—he tears the Achilles right off his heel. The tendon hovers in the air there for a moment, laughing at him, like a soul leaving the body after death.

It was so serious, none of the other players made fun of him. It was so serious, we even let him use the beer ice to ice it down—which violates about fourteen bylaws of our touch football league. Don't mess with the beer ice.

On Thursday, he had surgery.

Which is nothing compared with what happened to me when I asked Posh if she could wash the team jerseys, still sweaty days later and carrying a funky dad musk—motor oil, plus soggy cigar stubs, plus decaying human flesh.

A good stench, obviously. The scents of autumn.

She didn't greet this as eagerly as you might hope.

**Posh adds:**

*\*Go ahead.*

*\*\* In some ways, men act younger and younger as they age. I think it springs from their fear of death.*

**The columnist responds:**

*I think it springs from our fear of not having any fun.*

# "ANYTHING BOTHERING YOU?" THE DOCTOR ASKS

*April 10, 2010*

I'd rather go to a Clippers game than the doctor. I'd rather have my nose chewed off by zebras.

But still I go, if only for the very reasonable $20 co-payment. Really, you can't even get your oil changed for that.

So I roll into the doctor's office ten minutes early, a nasty habit. I arrive early almost everywhere. I was late for a dental appointment once, with the leggy Beverly Hills dentist, and I beat myself up about it for weeks. Some people are crazy for cleanliness. Me, I'm crazy for time.

See, I plan to live to be one hundred, a fine number if you're a cognac or a bowl game.* It's a little old for a martini-swilling American meatball like me. But I plan to live to be one hundred, if only to spite my children. The best revenge would be that, one day, they will actually have to diaper me.

Before you say, "Ewwwww," keep in mind all the stuff I've done for them, starting with prenatal care, bee stings, braces, college. I've taught them how to pack a cooler or re-lace a mitt. I've taught them the difference between Ecuador and Venezuela. They know Portugal is like the "left brain of Spain." On long car trips, I used to quiz them on the state capitals.

If you yourself know buckets of useless information, be sure to thank a dad, keepers of the trivial flame.

"Wally Pipp took a day off, and the rest is history," I reminded them the other day.

"Who's Wally Pipp?" one of them asked.

Evidently, my work is not yet done.

With that in mind, I'm getting a routine physical, a nice way to spend a sunny spring afternoon. My medical group's office—doctors travel in packs, like meerkats—is tucked into the side of the mountains, the kind of shadowy canyon where bandits used to hide. There's an In-N-Out Burger down the block that I suspect is owned by cardiologists. What a racket, medicine.

"You can go right in," the receptionist says. "Room Six."

This is my first doctor visit since the new health-care rules went into effect, and I can see the difference already. For one, they rush me into the exam room, probably so I can't debrief the other patients. One of my favorite things is waiting room conversations. "What are you in for?" Or, "Wow, is that a bunion?"**

I am a good patient, though, for I undress quickly and willingly, they never have to ask twice. There is no hesitation in the way I reveal myself. In an earlier life, I suspect I might've been a member of the British House of Lords.

"Good to see you," says Dr. Steve, holding out his hand. "Been a while."

Turns out, I am in peak physical form. My arms are like ship rope. You could bounce a tennis ball off my stomach—not high, but it would bounce a little, partly because, at fifty-three, I'm still built like a cedar chest, in the sense that I am hollow inside and repel moths.

"Ticklish?" the doctor says while pushing on my pancreas.

"No."

"That's okay, no extra charge," he says.***

Yeah, so I'm a little ticklish, big deal. I've always been an easy laugh. I laugh at funerals. I laugh at Kevin James movies. If laughter were a form of promiscuity, I'd be Italy.

"Anything bothering you?" Dr. Steve asks.

Well, doc, I'm not comfortable with the debt load the country is carrying right now. And there are too many medical dramas on TV, not to mention police procedurals—sick to death of those.

What else? Well, I wish I were more simpatico with my dog. Sometimes, it's as if he's in a completely different universe.

If anyone broke in, I'm pretty sure it's me he would attack. And I don't like the way he treats women.

"Well, my thumb is bothering me," I finally sputter.

"Can you bend it?"

"This much."

"It's probably just sprained," he says.

Then we talk about my prostate a while.

Let me just say this: I love my prostate. Half gland, half flower, it is more important to me than my brain or my heart—probably because I use it more.

Isn't it amazing how little love the prostate gets, considering it's importance in that very area. Nobody ever wrote a poem to his prostate.

For all their sonnets, did Keats or Shakespeare think to mention theirs once?

So let me be the first:

Roses are red, Viagra is blue,

I love my prostate, it's big as a shoe . . .

Actually, it might be bigger than a shoe, my doc says, not uncommon in men my age.

But it's healthy and mine, all mine—fifty-three going on forever. Under the new health regulations, I think I get to keep it.

**Dr. Steve responds:**

*\* One hundred is a big number and puts some pressure on me. I will point out that Chris has made it an additional seven years since this column was written. Every day is a gift.*

*\*\* I don't make my patients wait, and usually they like that. Chris feels he must suffer for his art and making him wait probably would have helped his creative process. (Note taken for future appointments.)*

*\*\*\* Adding a little levity to the exam can calm the patient down and help them get through an anxiety-provoking process. It works especially well with overly nervous creative types like movie stars, prima ballerinas, and print columnists.*

# THE FLOWER BOX

*October 25, 2014*

Just in time for fall, I build a nice flower box. That says so much about my life, I don't even know where to begin. A flower box in fall? Makes no sense whatsoever.

I'm not that good with my hands, but I need to use them anyway. Besides, only the human thigh is smoother than a nice piece of cabinet-grade redwood.

So I build a flower box.

A flower box pretty much exceeds my skills, which are better suited to backyard decks or framing closets—wham-bam projects that don't require a finish carpenter's steady touch. I double up on the old woodworker's credo that you measure twice and cut once.

I want to build this project inside the house, fuss over it in that sweet lazy hour just after dinner, or wrestle with it immediately after waking a little too early. But fearing it will be like one of those too-big boats that men build in their basements then can't get up the stairs, my wife insists I build the flower box outside, under the harsh glare of God.

I've had a problem with God lately. Two years ago, he took my friend Don Rhymer for no apparent reason, and there have been too many spotty performances since.

No one gets forever, but you should get more than fifty years. My pastor says we shouldn't expect God to give us more than he gave his own son—thirty-three years. But those were odd circumstances, softened by a showy resurrection.

So I'm still frosted and confused over Rhymer's death from cancer at age fifty-one. I'm dealing with it through this flower box.**

Some guys march to different drummers, others dance to their own minor keys.

That was Rhymer. His favorite retreat from the stupidities of screenwriting was a little cottage near the water, an apostrophe of a place, barely even there.

At this little Newport Beach cottage he would host summer holidays, build batches of margaritas, sizzle steaks on the grill. What a golf course was to Palmer, what Wembley was to Laver, this beach house was to Rhymer.

After he passed, buddies vowed to help his widow keep the place up against the effects of corrosive salt air, but there was nothing we could do for the rotting flower box out front. Better to build a new one at home, where I'd have sawhorses and power tools and the luxury of time.

I settled on a side of the house that got the afternoon shade. Went to work. Built a flower box. Remembered Rhymer.

The flower box is a triumph of Irish engineering, a little higher on one end than the other. A big believer in solid bottoms, I doubled the flooring, then smothered it in roofing tar to keep out the wet. What the flower box lacks in finesse, it makes up for in sheer heft. In a pinch, you could sail it to Korea.

You know, middle age comes to us on cat paws, then pounces. One day you're thirty-five and playing thirty-six holes, the next you're hearing your friends talk about hip replacements and exit strategies at work.

Look at the bright side, my friend: At least you didn't have to suffer that.

Damn, I miss you. Miss riffing about how nobody wears ascots anymore or owns a waterbed. Miss a sympathetic ear when I go on and on about how much I hate Shonda Rhimes shows.

"How do you think the American Revolution would've played out on social media?" I'd ask if he were still around.

And Rhymer would start riffing about Paul Revere's ride, or savage comments about the Redcoats.

"OMG, did you see what Thomas Gage was wearing?"

Two years later, I still need to chat him up like this, mock the fools who take themselves too seriously, vent about our spouses, catch up on the kids.

How rare is true friendship? How do you even build new friendships after a certain age?

Like this flower box, friendship is a loopy art form—misfit corners and lots of spackle.

Meanwhile, like Rhymer's memory, I can't let this flower box go. Where two coats of paint would do, I use three. Where a flat front would suffice, I add slight swells that mimic the ocean's waves, then sand the edges a little too much. Then a little more. For two weeks, my fingertips smell of trees.

Finally, I fill the box with flowers and leave it on the porch.

For you, old friend.

### * The columnist adds:
*Rhymer was fifty-one but looked and acted thirty-one. That's what made this so difficult to accept. Damn, I miss him.*

# THE AGONY OF DA FEET

*February 15, 2016*

I'd rather have my tongue waxed than run another marathon. If I ever suggest it, just gaff me, okay? Hoist me on my own petard. Shoot me in my knee because even that would be less painful than what I just went through.

*Marathon*, a Greek word meaning, "Oy, my aching ankles." No human being should run this far for free.

Heard over and over at the LA Marathon finish line Sunday: "This was the hardest thing I've ever done. Never doing this again."

You do remember the very first marathon killed Pheidippides, right? And he didn't even have to trudge up that nasty hill by the VA hospital. Somehow, the LA Marathon, despite ending at sea level, seems to have more uphill than down.

Let me show you my toes. Okay, skip the visual. I don't have very pretty feet to begin with, and now the left half of the left foot looks like the bloody finale of a Tarantino movie. When the race was over, I soaked the toes in the fountain at Tongva Park to stop them from cooking. No luck. I don't think I'll lose any nails. But the entire leg is a possibility.

Here's the menu of other health difficulties I suffered Sunday: heat stroke, dementia, swollen ankles, croup, malaria, tendinitis, strep throat, dehydration, chafed nipples, stretch marks, fistulas, and various rashes up and down my body. Or maybe those were old tattoos.

Thing is, the race started very well. At sunrise, about 21,000 sweaty soul mates and I left Dodger Stadium looking like the last wagon train heading west. The course bent this way and that way through Chinatown,

Echo Park, and a bunch of other places I generally try to avoid just because the parking is so lousy.

Real crowds didn't show until the runners reached Sunset Boulevard, where the live music and vocal spectators made it the most spirited and fun stretch of the twenty-six-million-mile course.

A radio host suggested one way to endure a long race like this is to dedicate each mile to a different person. So I dedicated the first one to Plaschke. The second one I dedicated to Shannon Farar-Griefer, an incredible ultramarathoner unable to compete this year because of multiple sclerosis. I dedicated miles three to five to my late buddy Don Rhymer, an incredibly wise guy who, were he still around, would've followed me in a rickshaw, bellowing like a coxswain: "Mush, you idiot. Mush."

See now why I miss him?

By the ninth mile, I was out of loved ones, so I started dedicating each segment to the girls who were extra nice to me in high school. That took me all the way to mile ten.

A few miles later, I found Jesus.

Marathon Jesus walks the course in robes, running shoes, and sunglasses nearly every year. This year, he said he left Dodger Stadium at midnight. By the time I caught up with him, he was at mile fourteen and had become a selfie sensation.

"Jesus, can we have a photo?" runners said.

"Hey, Jesus, can you turn this into wine?" a volunteer yelled while holding out a paper cup of water.

"Oh my God, it's Jesus!" cried another.

We palled around for a while, while I used my conversation with Jesus as an excuse not to run anymore, which I didn't really want to do anyway. If there's anything that can ruin a good marathon, it's running. I prefer to coast a little.

But when Marathon Jesus started asking me about the meaning

of life, I moved on.

My time? Six hours flat, only about four hours off what the winners did. The medal they gave me weighs more than my wife. You could melt it down and make a car. I think that's a sign they want me back. If I shave a minute here and there, I should be in contention next time.

If there is a next time. Probably not. Maybe. Despite the agony, there's just something about a race like this I admire.

Seems the most selfish of acts, a marathon. The logistics of getting a runner to the starting line, then home again, involves entire families, fleets of buses, thousands of volunteers waking up too early. Marathons are amazing things, really, a reflection of the esprit de corps of a city.

Only Pheidippides ever ran one alone. And look what happened to him.

# CUBS FINALLY WIN IT ALL

*November 4, 2016*

For fans of the impossible, the Chicago Cubs' World Series win late Wednesday night is a man-on-the-moon moment.

To be sure, it is a snide and upsetting planet we all share, and then for five hours Wednesday night it wasn't. An agonizing, wonderful, jagged Game Seven became the biggest sports story of the year, and one of the finest of our lifetimes.

I mean, the Cubs? Really? A trillion tweets, and I still don't believe it. Couldn't sleep the night before, couldn't sleep the night after. As a Chicago native, I feel caffeinated, buzzy, vindicated, sated. And so does anyone who ever picked the long shot, rooted for the Apaches, bet the mortgage on the underdog.

How momentous is this? The star-crossed Cubs are the champions of baseball. A virus, a curse, an anti-gravity has finally lifted from the land.

Could this come at a better time for a twitchy and divided nation? Amid so much troubling talk, we're all admiring baseball again, that stodgy, past-its-prime former national pastime. We're talking baseball again, after a World Series as sweet as Halloween candy. It was, quite probably, the most spectacular seven-game series we've ever witnessed.

The best thing about sports is how it can make you feel twelve again. I've followed this team for fifty-five years—not long, but certainly long enough. It's only a game, sure, and then sometimes it's everything. More than the sum of our hearts. As if religion married obsession.

For more than one hundred years, the Cubs have been the Great

American Metaphor for hope and unbridled optimism. Not often enough does faith like this get rewarded.

On Wednesday night in Cleveland, it finally did.

So many times, modern sports seems riddled with too many rascals and malcontents. The athletes are mostly just acting the way we would if we didn't pick up on social cues or fear what our mothers might say. The rascals are to be forgiven, mostly. We cheer their hubris and their wayward, bring-it-on demeanors.

But to really appreciate this moment, you have to understand Chicago, if that's possible. It's an angry city with—until now—a giant hole in its chest. The weather is awful, the elevated trains all squeak. This time of year, the whole city starts to rust.

It's a city that produces more big-fisted literary lions and lousy quarterbacks than it does World Series champs. It's always too quick to fight.

In fact, in the year the Cubs last accomplished this, 1908, one player threw ammonia in another player's face and then was beaten to a pulp by the manager, Frank Chance.

The Cubs are no poetry society is what I'm saying, yet they couldn't crack the mysterious code that wins a World Series. There are 108 stitches in a baseball, and it was 108 years since they last won a championship. A Buddhist mala has 108 beads, signifying all our mortal desires.

Yeah, it's all religion and numerology and things we'll never quite fathom. Fittingly, the Cubs didn't keep it simple on Wednesday night— have they ever?

Just like players can press too hard, so can managers. The Cubs skipper yanked his starter too soon, overused his closer, botched a bunt on a three-two count with one out and the winning run on third.

True, sometimes the best coaching move is the one no one sees coming. Home runs usually win ball games like this, not bunts.

Now we see why.

In the end, the real hero became an audaciously cerebral pinch-runner who tagged and took second on a deep fly ball—another thing we never see.

So now the curse is broken, the anti-gravity is gone, and we have firm evidence of a benevolent God.

Don't forget team alchemist Theo Epstein, forty-two, who has now accomplished the impossible in Boston and Chicago, two cursed cities. With this, the boy genius elevates himself to best sports exec of all time and one of the finest in any field. EPSTEIN FOR PRESIDENT signs will probably dot the Cubs' victory parade.

For on a soppy November night in Cleveland, the former San Diego law student again elevated this grand old game from a niche sport to something glorious again.

Be still, our baseball hearts. We all just touched the moon.

# HOW MANY KIDS IS BEST?

*August 6, 2011*

Young couples are always asking me: "What's the ideal number of kids?" To which I wisely reply: zero. Then they laugh, assuming I (the father of four) must be messing with them.

"Consider a dog instead," I say, because they never roll their eyes, have no interest in attending college, and are more selective about whom they date.

Dogs don't need braces. You don't have to buckle them into car seats, or watch their school plays, which are tremendously overrated. Some of that kindergarten scenery is so cheesy. The character interpretations are over the top. Really, you call that art?

With dogs, you'll never find yourself speeding in the fast lane in a minivan, late for trombone practice. You'll never have to watch them pack a suitcase.

Ever see an eight-year-old pack a suitcase? What he'll do is grab an armful of the closest clothes he can find—ski jackets, Halloween costumes. Then he'll cram the clothes into the suitcase with his knee. Umuuuuuumph.*

The stuff he can't fit—the spillover—he stuffs under his bed. Then he congratulates himself on his excellent packing skills, for he has done in seconds what it takes his prickly mother two days to do.

Nice job. Yay, me.

The little guy and I took a road trip the other day, and all these things about children were apparent again.

"We're not having breakfast?" he asks one morning, so I take him to a café, where he colors the kids' menu and never touches his food. At any given meal, he is more likely to eat the crayons than the Mickey Mouse pancake.

"Can I have dessert?" he asks when he is finished not eating his breakfast.

"You don't have dessert with breakfast," I remind him.

"Mom lets me," he lies.

"Do you have another mom?" I ask. "Because the mother I know would never give you dessert with breakfast."

We're in Arizona on a short road trip. Don't ask me why. I guess California wasn't hot enough for us, so we thought we'd give Phoenix a try.

We really like it.

Know what the state animal of Arizona is? The blown-out tire. The rubber remnants line the fry-pan freeways like roadkill. It makes for a very nice entrance to this enchanted kingdom, and I wish more cities would use it.

At noon Friday, on the radio, they play "The Star-Spangled Banner" (I'm really serious). Apparently the national anthem is still a Top Ten song in Arizona. "The Battle Hymn of the Republic" is probably right up there, too.

"It's one hundred degrees at the airport right now," the weathercaster says during the 9:30 p.m. newscast.

I look out the window to see if anyone is still alive.

Lots of bunnies in Scottsdale. Lots of FOR SALE signs too. The only parks appear to be these things they call golf courses, which are everywhere. Apparently, that's where the bunnies live and copulate, as well as most of the people, whose ears twitch from the heat just like those of the rabbits.

At 4 p.m. one day, the little guy spots his first UFO. "Look, Dad, a spaceship!"**

At 4:01 p.m., I feel the need to start drinking.

Earlier, I'd tried to pull from a finger some tiny cactus thistles—skinny things you could barely see, like tiny blond actresses.

Of course, I used my teeth to extract the harmless little thistles because that's a tool we cowboys use a lot—our teeth—and the next thing I know, the thistles are embedded in my tongue.

Yum.

Now I know why cowboys spit so much.

Anyone can have a bad day, especially me, so I follow through on my urge to drink and order a margarita about the size of an Arabian horse. It comes in one of those margarita containers that sort of, kind of, resembles a glass.

It's not like me to criticize, but let us pause a moment to consider the utter ridiculousness of the iconic margarita glass, the wobbliest vessel since Nick Nolte.

A margarita glass is dumb in the way top-heavy things often are. There is no steady place to hold it—no balance point—the way you hold a football or a good six-shooter.

Perhaps if there were no gravity, if our fingers were less tremulous with the worries of the world, a margarita glass might be a fine thing to drink from.

But there is gravity, there is stress, and in this increasingly demanding world, I challenge anyone to devote the proper resources to redesigning the basic margarita glass. It's almost an emergency.

Thanks for listening (I'm really serious).

Or, as someone with cactus in his tongue might put it: "I'm weally therious."

\* The little guy responds:
*Is that me? Is it?*

The columnist answers:
*Duh.*

\*\* The little guy says:
*It was like a black dot falling from the sky. What else could it be?*

The columnist answers:
*Your suitcase?*

# TIPS FOR A NEWCOMER TO LA

*July 22, 2017*

My twenty-six-year-old niece is moving here soon, so I've made a few notes for her about life in Los Angeles:

Dear Amy,

I'm looking forward to your arrival. I want to warn you that Southern California is a little different. For instance, it is the only American city strung together by beach volleyball nets. Like vertebrae, they form a skeletal underpinning that protects us from earthquakes. Mostly it works.

As you know from visits, LA is a diverse place—in activities, in skin tone, in temperament. It is the land of Richard Nixon and Jane Fonda, of Silicon Beach and the Warner's lot. Volleyball nets form its spine, and so do freeways. You'll find that there is a freeway to everywhere, except the places everyone needs to go—Fairfax and 3rd or West Hollywood.

Before you come, be sure to read your Chandler. Be sure to read your Nathanael West. They were both sort of right about Los Angeles.

"From thirty feet away she looked like a lot of class," Chandler once wrote. "From ten feet away she looked like something made up to be seen from thirty feet away."

And Amy, that pretty much sums up your adopted new town.

The challenge and the glory of Los Angeles is that it changes so fast that it defies definition. You can't really chronicle LA, except maybe in a tweet. LA was built in one hour, on a very hot Friday afternoon.

Change is life, change is grand. When you find a place in LA with a sense of history, maybe some exposed brick, appreciate it—because they're about to tear it down.

That's the flip side of progress, of idealism, of a restless and creative spirit.

In LA, unlike in other big cities, nobody recognizes the City Council members, no matter how badly they screw things up. There are more homeless people out here than trees.

We are a town of thundering special effects and no weather. There is rarely a cloud in LA. The river is empty, but the ocean stays pretty full.

When it does rain, everyone rejoices and then skids off the road. Once every two years, someone uses a turn signal.*

Cars are what we mostly worship, but you'll find many religious choices here, too. Approximately twenty percent of LA residents believe in unicorns. Some thirty percent believe in hobbits. Only five percent believe in a benevolent God.

Oh, I jest because after living here for nearly thirty years, I love LA and its open minds . . . its empty minds, and every now and then, its very brilliant minds. In LA, you'll run across the smartest people you'll ever meet, and they'll probably be driving for Uber.

Still, it is a magnificent and inspiring place—America's shining city on a hill. You'd have to move to Monaco to find mountains this close to beaches or wild animals this close to ingenues. In the foothills, we keep black bears as pets.

Los Angeles is absolutely a wonderful place to eat. For a few bucks, you can get fish tacos with a tangy sauce you can't identify. Or, for $300, you can have a sit-down dinner at Totoraku, a restaurant without a sign.

This is the place where fusion meets fusion, where Asia meets America, where good marries evil, then immediately begins to see other people. If you live right, most of the time you will have seawater in your hair. Most of the year, your bare feet will have a leathery bottom, as if it is always summer.

It isn't.

All that "endless summer" stuff comes from the 1950s and '60s. The bohemian vibe from that time is slipping away, quashed by gentrification and surprisingly long workweeks. The only thing endless about LA now is the talk of making LAX better, which we never will.

LAX is our failed welcome mat and proof that we don't really care about what outsiders think.

Amy, you know that awkward moment when someone in the audience starts a standing ovation but no one joins them? You see that a lot in LA. It defines the sweet but obstinate nature of our town. Here, even school plays don't necessarily receive standing ovations. Even as a third grader, you have to "earn it."

In that sense, Los Angeles is a very tough town. As I tell my kids: "Don't be nice, there's no future in it."

Yet, your cousins grew up here and have managed to stay very nice, as have most of the people we know. Strangers on the street are genuinely nice. That person on the next bar stool, or at the table next to you at the Farmers Market, might be from Chile or Germany, or Prague or Peoria.

And they'll have a smile and a nod for you, and an interesting story to share.

Soon, like Chandler and West, you will, too.

**\* The columnist adds:**
*On her third day here, Amy got in a fender bender. Nothing serious.*
*A fist bump. A love tap. We do that with all the newcomers.*

# WHY HER?

# THE UNANSWERABLE QUESTION

*February 11, 2017*

Routine day. Used the last of the Christmas stamps to pay some bills. The mortgage, for one. I bank online, but for some reason prefer to mail in the mortgage, a tactile celebration. Like reading a good newspaper.

The afternoon rain was steady and now routine. The new puppy liked going out to lick at puddles. Amid the downpour, I cursed the leak over the kitchen stove. Last thing you need after the holidays, right?

But as I told the kids, don't bemoan a leaky roof. Be thankful you have a roof. And a puppy who thinks puddles are full of free champagne.

We finally settled in on a dreary day to watch a little football. Other than the leaky roof, my biggest gripe was the way the cheese spread wouldn't smear on a cracker.

A few hours later, Posh and I were in the emergency room, where we realized that there are no real problems except for health problems.

"I'm afraid I have some bad news . . ." the ER doctor began.

Bad news? We'd only been in the emergency room for an hour or two, long enough for them to run a few scans on my exhausted wife and draw some blood, which the tech admitted looked "a little thin."

Bad news? It wasn't until a week earlier that my wife had started feeling poorly and complained of abdominal pain. Even then, a little fever, some nausea . . . maybe the flu? The only alarming thing was that she had shed too much weight and looked, on some days, as pale as a paper towel.

But we figured that was her anemia, a genetic trait that could leave her feeling run-down. In the last few weeks, she hadn't so much as coughed.

So when the doctor we barely knew told us Posh had cancer, in the uterus and in the lungs, we were the two most shocked people on the planet.

Cancer. There had been mercifully little of it in her family. There had been bad tickers and diabetes, but not cancer.

I'd lost my dad to the world's worst disease and, five years ago, a great and irreplaceable friend. Almost lost my buddy Paul to cancer two years ago.

Paul reminded us that cancer never calls ahead. "No one thinks their aching elbow is bone cancer," he said. "No one thinks a headache is a tumor."

At such times, you can't think of anything but the stunning diagnosis. How far along is it? What are her chances? What are you not telling us?

In the next few days, with all the biopsies and additional tests, we learned little else except that it is an aggressive cancer and that surgery was ahead, then chemo.

*Cancer* is our most-frightening word, followed by *chemo*, which can be as disabling as the disease it sets out to crush.

But first, there was the abdominal surgery. The wunderkind surgeon came highly recommended. But was that enough? I didn't want a doctor. I wanted God.

She was admitted to a comfortable room with a view of the storms. Behind all those clouds, Mt. Wilson. Nothing smelled of the outdoors, though. Her pillows were industrial, like the ones you get on planes. Suddenly, her life was tubes and get-well cards and lab techs poking around for another vein.

She seemed to have one hundred physicians and a new nurse every hour. Some of her doctors were timid and incoherent; others, bold and cold. A few were sensational. One told us she wanted to be a dermatologist. Great. Because zits are a big concern for us right now.

And there my wife rests, the woman with the Marlo Thomas eyes and feet like Cinderella. Like other couples, she and I have had our problems, but now we are a team again.

We'll beat this, baby. No doubts at all.

Yet, "Why her?" I keep asking. I'm the one who lives like a sailor on shore leave, who mocks kale and anything regarded as "healthful."

"Why her?" I'm the one who misbehaves, doesn't read food labels, and wraps myself in bacon and bad wine.

Why her, over three decades, one of the most devoted mothers you ever saw, very nearly a saint.

As all this plays out—the IVs, the prognoses, the second opinions— that's the question that haunts me.

For the love of God, why her?

### The older daughter adds:

*For a family that had largely stayed out of hospitals and emergency rooms—no broken bones, minor head bumps, a few scratches—this was the shock of a lifetime. To be honest, my dad shared this in the paper well before I had been able to tell many close friends. I hadn't been able to find the words. I learned very quickly that there was no easy way to share news like this. While I didn't know how to talk about it, my dad was able to put words to explain such a senseless situation. This article proved to be an easy way to share the heartbreak with many people, and I realized how big our community is—so many people come out of the woodwork to share their love and support. Sadly, when this happens in your family, you become part of a not-very-exclusive club that has zero applicants. Talking about it opens people's hearts and arms and makes you feel not so alone. My dad's words in this article helped move that process along—bringing a reality to light, making it much easier to talk about, and helping us to accept the support of others through these tough times.*

# CHEMO BAY NO. 8

*March 4, 2017*

Of all the popular poisons, chemo is my favorite. The oddest of medicines, it beats you down as it fixes you up in hopes that it will eventually save your mortal soul.

Results are mixed. Prayer and single-malt Scotch might be more effective. Actually, you need a little of all three.

Greetings from chemo bay No. 8 in the cancer annex of a local hospital. We're squeezed into a corner cubicle, about the size of your office's coffee nook. I asked for the honeymoon suite and this is what we wound up with. Never had much luck with upgrades. Or honeymoons.

At least there's a TV. Fussy nurses dart in and out like point guards. My wife, Posh, has a blanket, heated in some oven. I have lukewarm coffee. And her again.

I have not seen my spouse this much since the first week we dated. As then, she is tiny, maybe ninety-five pounds. Her chestnut hair is thinner now, but she still has those killer cheekbones and the cutest dimple—like an apostrophe—on just one side of her smile.

These days, we share every meal. I fear she will tire of me soon . . . her constant shadow, her pharmacist, her masseur, her own personal comedian/coach, who she confessed isn't particularly funny after all.

For now, she is stuck with me. Her fate rests, in part, in the hands of a wise guy who can barely work a digital thermometer. "What was so wrong with the old thermometers?!" I shout. (I find myself growing angry at a lot of stupid stuff.) Why does everything now need batteries? Or when did pills become "meds"?

That's a tangent, sure, but the tangents save me. I talk of cancer so much that a brief conversation about the Lakers or the price of rib eyes keeps me on the safer side of sane. Tuesday, I did a five-minute bit on how Meryl Streep movies always put me to sleep.

And what could be more all-consuming than this? We are in week two of her chemo treatments. When finished, she'll have had eighteen total innings, at which time she will have won.

Or so we hope. At this moment, a bag of Benadryl hangs from a stainless steel hook to be followed by the special sauce: Taxol.

The Taxol, with a carboplatin boost, is supposed to rinse the lesions from her lungs and some post-surgical cancer lower in her hull. The specialists have high hopes, to be sure, though nothing with this type of cancer comes with guarantees. No refunds, no returns. You get more assurances when you buy a $30 toaster.

Meanwhile, Posh's oncology nurse is the most important woman in her life since her mother. For these weekly sessions, her nurse (Kathy) greets her at the reception desk, and they go arm and arm down the hallway, old chums who have known each other all of two weeks.

I trail behind, carrying her *Vogue* and her slipper socks. I look like hell, not that it matters much. I need a haircut and a face-lift. In the mirror, Kurt Vonnegut stares back—bad mustache, worse hair. Pale and verklempt. Ice cubes have more color. "Hey, nurse, I might need a transfusion here."

Now that I'm not funny anymore, appearance is more important than ever.

For humor, which everyone insists is so damn important, we've turned to other members of the comedy troupe. Posh laughs at how the blue-eyed Siberian, still a puppy, licks the sap off the firewood, or how our daughter arranged the avocados "chronologically, according to ripeness," knowing we won't eat all three of them the same day.

I'm just glad our daughter isn't overthinking things.

At home, we fight the cancer with food. The nutritionist orders six-ty-five grams of protein a day, which I believe is roughly equivalent to ten sides of beef. Or, as I've always called it: lunch.

As I keep telling the kids, "If she opens her mouth to yawn, send in a slab of veal."

The other day, a neighbor dropped off a fresh-baked pie so good, Posh sighed, "Oh gawwwd!" at the first forkful. Equally divine, there have been stews and casseroles and Croatian brownies. Love may be the best bubble wrap, but ancient family recipes run a close second.

Then, one day: lasagna.

Half Sicilian, Posh has been cooking lasagna since she was three. Her version is seven layers deep, as thick as a good quilt and built with the same care craftsmen put into a Lamborghini.

Not knowing this, one friend delivered the large tray of lasagna. It would be like taking lilies to Monet.

Turns out, that lasagna was a terrific call. She jumped on it like a shark, as did the rest of her comedy troupe. Mussolini never ate so well.

One morsel at a time—a hearty pasta, a plate of steak—we are filling her out like this, making her robust again.

You know, she was always prettiest when she was pregnant.

# THE BABY HUMMINGBIRD

*March 11, 2017*

Friends keep asking, "What do you guys need? What do you guys need?" and I always respond: tequila, stock tips, and those "nubby little cigars that bookies chew like cannoli." They laugh as if I'm kidding.

I shrug and go back to caring for Posh, which is a little like being the executive assistant to a demanding studio mogul. Sure, the pay is modest and the hours are merciless, but you get to be around greatness.

"There's another narcissist here to see you," I announce.

"Who?" Posh asks.

"Your son," I say.

Or it could be a daughter or one of the dogs or one of the Chardonnay Moms, who drop in for lunch to check on how their dear friend is progressing.

"Send him in anyway," she says of her son.

One day at a time, we deal with cancer. Some weeks, we have five medical appointments, occasionally two in one day. With her in the backseat, I drive to all of them, avoiding potholes, sudden stops, and police standoffs.

Ever tried that on an LA freeway? It's like a video game. It's like driving across a breakwater of broken toasters.

I could complain, but I won't.

Smooth driving is imperative because Posh is bone-weary from three weeks of chemo. She suffers every little bump. In my defense, I explain that I haven't driven this carefully since we ferried our third and last baby home from the hospital.

"Um, we had four," she says.

"Seriously?"

"Yes," she says.

No wonder there's never enough cake.

Mostly, we don't mind these little outings. They are vital to her recovery and a chance to get out of the house. Daytime TV is worse than boring; it's belligerent. If the insipid talk shows don't eat your brain, the food shows will. Me, I'd rather chew a wad of aluminum foil than watch one more episode of *Diners, Drive-Ins, and Dives*.

I mean, what's the big deal about dives? We live in one.

Speaking of cooking shows, I got in trouble the other day for reorganizing a kitchen drawer.

It was making me nuts the way the utensil drawer would jam at six in the morning, when all I was trying to do was make the little guy a few eggs before school.

What would happen is I'd open the drawer for the spatula, and a whisk or a turkey baster would jam the over-stuffed drawer, so I'd have to tug-tug-tug . . . curse . . . tug-tug-tug before I could eventually clear it.

"You gotta take care of yourself" is another thing I keep hearing from friends.

*I have to take care of everything,* is what I think to myself.

Life being what it is, my wife and daughter didn't really appreciate that I reorganized this drawer. It wasn't so much that it worked better that annoyed them; it was my audacity at doing it without their blessing, which is something I would never get anyway, so I just went ahead and did it. I think of it as Hannibal attacking at the Trebia.

Anyway, the reorganized drawer is working smoothly, and now they don't so much trust me around the kitchen, where the cereal cabinet might be next. Trust me, there are cereals in there that predate oxygen.

I could complain, but I won't.

"Be sure to take care of yourself," someone texts.

Yeah, but first I have to feed the baby hummingbird.

As you've learned, our place has long been a landing pad for misfits and lost souls, so it's no wonder that the homeless hummingbird found her way to our front porch. When you have three or four children, what's one more mouth?

Thing is, I never really liked hummingbirds. Tiny and operatic in their movements, they seem to make life look too easy. If there's anything I know about life, it's that it's never too easy.

Anyway, one morning the Siberian puppy was in the yard, praying for snow, when she nosed something that nosed her back. It was a newborn bird, as small as your belly button.

Unable to find the nest, the older boy scooped the hummingbird into a shallow box. For four days, we have fed her sugar water from an old toothbrush.

She seemed to like me, this hummingbird. I suspect it was my mustache or my skinny jeans, or maybe her eyesight was still a little smeary. No matter. Tony Soprano had his ducks; I have this homeless baby hummingbird.

It's a small joy, but as one reader put it, "Everything looks different with cancer."

Almost hourly—and a tad miraculously—her birth mother still comes to feed her. This must be confusing for the young bird. In her mind, she must think she has two moms: the gorgeous green angel and me, the idiot with the old toothbrush.

She could complain. But she won't.

# POSH IS BACK

*June 10, 2017*

"Dad, I love you," one of the kids said the other day.

I thought to myself, *Yeah? What's the catch?*

As I warned another parent recently, just assume your teenagers are lying to you. When they happen to tell the truth—which occurs occasionally—you can always adjust accordingly.

Just to be safe, I've been doing background checks on every member of the family as well as an audit of their souls. What I find is troubling.

For instance, this new dog our son brought home . . . well, I think she's really a wolf. Oh, you can call her a "Siberian husky," but that's merely a fancy label. She's a wolf, pure and simple. Smells like a wolf, moves like a wolf. Chewed my best leather belt like a wolf.

Let me give you an example: Marilyn Monroe could dye her hair the color of cumulus clouds, add some wiggle and a sparkly gown, and she was still just Norma from Van Nuys.

Same with this new puppy. You can dress her up, but she's still just a wolf in a nice designer dress.

Case clothed. Let's move on.

Surprisingly, the only one to pass the background check was Posh, whom I've been suspicious of for a very long time. Four months ago, my wife put her fate in the hands of a man whose favorite song is the theme from *MASH*, who understands baseball's infield-fly rule far better than he does the stock market or net neutrality or how yeast works.

Emotionally, I'm still at a stage where the right Jethro Tull song on the radio can make me late for work. And as my daughter noted recently: "Dad, your lips move when you text."

What kind of person puts her faith in someone like that?

Well, the doctors had said "cancer, stage four," so I suppose Posh was a little desperate. I was there to help, and as eager as a dumb puppy. I didn't feel responsible for her cancer, just every other challenge in her life: the plain little ranch house, the minivan with the "check-engine" light aglow, the dryer that kept scorching the shirts. Most of all, a topsy-turvy marriage.

The least I could do in the face of her diagnosis was get her to the appointments, fill her meds, keep the dogs fed, change the furnace filter, chase fur balls with a broom, tarp the leaky roof. Trust me, it was not as thrilling as I make it sound.

Bad as all that was, she had cancer, which is worse than about anything else that can ever happen. How could I gripe about the missing tax records—or anything—when she was enduring injections, transfusions, lab tests, fatigue, nausea, and hair loss? A good day was one where they didn't poke her with a four-inch needle.

Her secret weapons were a Wonder Woman oncologist (take a bow, Lynda Roman), a rock-star chemo nurse (take a bow, Kathy Dressler), and a warrior spirit. Not once did Posh complain.

Her other secret weapons were four very supportive children, one of whom moved back home from Cincinnati to help, and a wolf/husky that kept her laughing with her puppy antics. Lastly, chasing fur balls with an old broom, was me.

As I've mentioned, my wife doesn't find me funny at all, but I haven't told her the new R-rated joke about the pickle slicer (email me, and I'll share).

Her final and very effective secret weapons were the thousands of prayers, the meals dropped off on the porch, the gift cards, the books from

Pastor Chuck, the lawn guys Parker sent over, the hand-knit caps from the reader in Temple City, the inspiring cards and notes from all over the map.

Thank you. We are not out of the woods yet: eleven chemo sessions behind us, six to go. But the results have been remarkable. Four months ago, she could barely get up off the couch. Yesterday, she walked five miles just because.

And now as I do inventories, and audits of the soul, their mother is back to scurrying around the house, using barbecue tongs to pick up her sons' repulsive socks, scolding the dogs, mocking me for making a margarita using her favorite crystal vase.

Hey, I just want to toast her properly.

"My ears hurt from listening to you, and it's not even the first day of summer," she told the little guy the other day.

Posh is back, all right. Cheers to everyone.

# I STOP FOR LIGHTHOUSES

*September 23, 2017*

I don't even know what dreams I have left. They are diaphanous, semi-formed, and live under the stairs. When I was thirty, I had a long list of dreams.

At sixty, they are written in highlighter on the back of my hand. You can barely make them out: I dream about my wife getting healthy, my kids being content.

Unfortunately, contentment is nothing we really preach. Our nation started as Pilgrims, and we are now a jump-up-and-down, I-won-the-lottery sort of society. We lust for uncool things: fame, fortune, fashion, faster phones. . . .

Trust me, finding contentment is winning the lottery.

Been a funny week. My sister in Chicago misspelled my name on a check (it used to be her last name, too). How quickly they forget.

And I finally sold the Camaro, a car that had been for sale for seven years and was about to be buried in the backyard.

I lost my phone charger, then found it, then lost it again. Everything seemed misplaced. Two idiots wouldn't return my calls. The 300-pound beagle wouldn't take his kidney meds no matter what.

"You need to be more patient," Posh suggested.

"I invented patience!!!" I screamed.

What followed was a twenty-minute argument over whether I invented patience. Which I did.

So when my buddy Siskin invited me up the coast for a day or two, my wife was glad to let me go.

Off I went, in a cheesy rental car, ugly as a fire truck, on airless tires that rattled over every road seam. Stopped at Rincon Beach, then stopped for a steak so massive, it should've come with a bell around its neck.

Just before sunset, I rolled into Cayucos, which is below Cambria but lots less artsy. If there's anything I like about a place, it's that it is less artsy.

Wow, what a place Siskin rented. Not that it was big—I'm so done with mansions. I can barely afford the one I have.

Siskin's place was just right, with a living room that zoomed out to the sea. Perched on a bluff, it wasn't a house so much as a hang glider.

Like me, Siskin is a talker. We talked about books and the troubled relationship between hope and truth. We talked about the Clippers, the future of football, the birds bristling along the beach.

Siskin was certain they were snowy plovers. To me, they looked like common gulls with gym memberships—a little sleeker, a little more careful about what they ate.

"Yep, those are plovers," Siskin insisted.

No one can quite explain my buddy Siskin. Or the ocean either. There are all sorts of theories about the positive vibes released by crashing waves or the psychic rewards of staring at the horizon.

Part of the reason California is such an asylum is that it is full of people who fixated on horizons, then set off to explore them. I like that in a place.

As the sun set, we sat on the deck and watched a parade of sea creatures. Is that an otter or a seal? No one could tell. Might've been a surfer. This far north, even the sea lions wear wet suits.

In the distance, humpbacks spewed. Close to shore, a family of dolphins slipped through the waves; they were shiny, as if just painted.

Who doesn't love dolphins? Do they deserve it? What have they really done? To me, a dolphin is a celebrity without merit, the Macaulay Culkin of the sea.

Siskin's wife, Jenny, joined us, and we took long walks to nowhere. After that, we ate all the oysters in the ocean.

Immediately, I felt better.

Eating an oyster, Tom Robbins once noted, is like "French-kissing a mermaid," so we ordered way too many. You either love oysters or you don't. Jenny watched in horror, but she was a good sport about it. She hurled only twice.

After the hike, the September sun was warm on our necks and our legs still burned.

Amid its difficulties, God still has a crush on California. It has restorative powers that we often take for granted. There is medicine in the sunlight.

And, in California, the year gets better with every month, not worse, as in most states. September is better than August, and October is even better than September.

If I had my way, October would be ninety days long. Yet November is even better. Leave it said we'll enjoy a damn fine harvest.

Later, I drove farther up the coast to do my usual dorky activities— lingering too long over lighthouses and eating too much rhubarb pie.

Like oceans, no one has ever sufficiently explained our love of lighthouses. Probably Longfellow came closest, noting that lighthouses are "steadfast, serene . . . a quenchless flame."

Really, aren't we all?

### The columnist adds:

*Helluva year. As I wrote this, we'd just discovered that Posh had to go back on the sauce: chemo. She was feeling fine but the aggressive cancer had returned. The outlook is still bright. We're still very hopeful. And that's what these lighthouses—these quenchless flames—represent to me.*

# ACKNOWLEDGMENTS

Posh and the kids, who gamely share their lives each week and contributed many of the tailpieces at the end of the columns.

The *Los Angeles Times,* which was good enough to hire me twenty-eight years ago, a leap of faith on the editors' part, but one that has worked out very well for me—most of the time.

Colleen Dunn Bates, the visionary at Prospect Park Books, who saw the value in this collection and made the process a complete pleasure. It was her idea to add the tailpieces, a terrific touch. Her colleagues there, Dorie Bailey and Caitlin Ek, and book designer David Ter-Avanesyan.

I have no book agent. But if I did, it would be Allison Cohen, of the Gersh Agency, who looked over the contract and gave me excellent guidance.

My editors over the years at the *Times,* the *Chicago Tribune, The Washington Post, The Denver Post,* the *Pittsburgh Post-Gazette,* and other papers across the country, which, faced with a leaf pile of stories every single day, managed to pull my stuff from the stack and treat it well.

Cherished readers, hiking club members, my two sassy sisters, and bartenders across the nation who slipped me an extra drink now and then.

Jack, Paul, Bittner, Siskin, Howard, Dr. Steve, Eugene, Pete, T-Bone, Big Wave Dave, Billable Bob, Charlie, Stanton, Commie, Jeff, Curwen, Reynolds, Hamm, Harnagel, Lynch, and the rest of my funny friends.

And finally, to my own late father, who gave me the greatest gift: a sense of humor no matter what.

Thank you.

## ABOUT THE AUTHOR

Chris Erskine is a longtime humor columnist who mines the rich worlds of fatherhood, marriage, and suburbia; his columns are featured weekly in the *Los Angeles Times* and *Chicago Tribune*, and they also appear sometimes in many papers, including the *Buffalo News, Orlando Sentinel, Arizona Republic*, and *Pittsburgh Post-Gazette*. The father of four and resident of a quiet LA suburb, Erskine is also a staff editor and writer at the *Los Angeles Times*, as well as the author of two previous books, *Man of the House* and *Surviving Suburbia*.